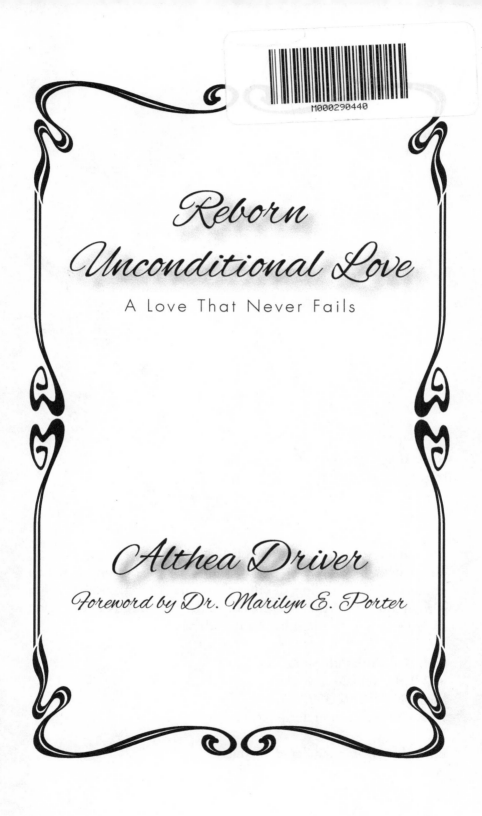

Reborn Unconditional Love

A Love That Never Fails

Althea Driver

Foreword by Dr. Marilyn E. Porter

ISBN 978-1-0980-7731-0 (paperback)
ISBN 978-1-0980-7732-7 (digital)

Christian Faith Publishing, Inc.
832 Park Avenue
Meadville, PA 16335
www.christianfaithpublishing.com

Printed in the United States of America

Foreword

MY ENCOUNTER WITH ALTHEA MADE it very clear that she is a ball of Holy Ghost joy, smiles, accompanied by an energy that was unmatched in any room—just good folk, as they say in the Deep South.

In that moment, I did not know her story (her history). I did not meet an addict. I did not encounter a homeless woman. I had no indication of the woes and hardships that she had been exposed to because she did not look like, sound like, or smell like what she'd been through. To God be the glory for this precious living testimony that you will come to know as Ms. Althea Driver.

I myself grew up amid many of the ills of society that Althea endured in her life, and I survived by grace. I understand drug and alcohol addictions from an outsider's view. I will admit that Althea's words have given me an insider's view of the disease of addiction. I now know how to pray for those battling this demon of addiction, because Althea has opened my heart and led me to compassion in a way that growing up in a drug=infested neighborhood in New Jersey had not done before.

The Lord blessed me to share in the processing of this book in such a deeper way that I had anticipated. It allowed me to become an admirer of the woman with the pen in her hand. At times in my own mind, there would be conflict, because I was reading the story (the past) while getting to know the woman on the other side of the story (the present). Yes, I was literally meeting the whole Althea Driver through the testimony she is releasing in these pages and the voice of a healthy, whole, and healed woman of God.

The book, this book that you are preparing to indulge in, is for sure a life-changing encounter. Althea gives you full access to the truth of who she was, is, and shall be according to the workings of Jesus Christ. Redemption is the message, and healing is the outcome. She has written words of strength that will penetrate your being if you open your heart and receive them as healing waters.

Reborn, Unconditional Love: A Love That Never Fails is a healing balm. Addiction may not be your story—at least not the one that you identify with. I urge you to search your own heart and see if there is anything in your life that you give more time to. Restoration and healing is something that every human being alive stands in the need of at some point in life. So be prepared to dig deeper inside yourself. Allow the Holy Spirit to speak to your heart, as Althea shares her heart, her truth, her God-ordained testimony. Be mindful that this is how we overcome by the power of our testimony, as per Revelation 12:11 (read it for yourself and be set free).

I thank you, Ms. Althea Driver, for standing naked and unashamed before the world, that others might be set free!

—Dr. Marilyn E. Porter

Pastor, publisher, life coach

www.marilyneporter.com

# Introduction

My story is a story of growth and the need to change. As I look back from where I have come from the glory of my younger years, wishing I knew then what I know now I have faced myself and all the pain that comes with it. I realized that change wasn't going to happen until I started making changes in my life. Some people have seen from where God has brought me to where I am now. I have faced a lot of adversities. I am an overcomer who is grateful for everything. I am blessed to, most importantly, have my life. I am grateful to be here to share my story reaching out to those who are bound by addictions and to instill within them the hope that is needed to reclaim their power.

I am thankful for the gracious favor of God that is upon my life. I have longed to share with you some of the things I have gone through and the pain I have endured. So much wasted time, so many stupid mistakes that I had made that I could not make over. I now realize I was not ready for what was yet to come in my life until the appointed time. I have settled into the paradox of getting older, and you realize that in your slowing down, you're more prepared to listen to things you were moving too fast before to hear. On the one hand, I finally have some sense about what I'm doing in the world. And most of all, I'm convinced I have a right to be here. I no longer fear the past, I cannot tell whether it's because I've evolved or just aged. The one thing I have learned on this journey is after my conscious awakening I never wanted to go back to person I once were. The only way we can be happy is be willing to take responsibility for our actions and our experiences. God has been faithful to me. He promised that He would never leave me nor forsake me. It is truly a blessing for me to share the love of God and how He delivered me. I am forever grateful to be a blessing.

I am much more confident in myself today that I have come to a place and time in my life that I can share my story with others in a way that it will be a blessing to them as well. I cannot keep what has happened to myself any longer. I must share things that I have experienced on this journey. You cannot imagine what I've gone through being an addict, an alcoholic, and a homeless person for the past twenty years. The pain of addiction and the strongholds that once tormented me when I didn't know where I was and when I lost my way, only later to realize that the Father was there to remind me where I was. When I needed to find a place of refuge, He was there to guide me and to remind me I am His child.

My story is a testimony to the world. I know that to some of you it may not seem like such a big deal, but for me, it has been a life-changing experience that I will always remember. My story is about sharing a part of me that needs to be told. I am not looking for any special favors or sympathy, for I am filled with gratitude. I believe and know that I can stand today and say that I am delivered! I am free from condemnation, guilt, and shame. I am truly blessed and highly favored because I have been reborn by His unfailing love. I can finally understand the excitement was not out there it was within when I consciously choose to see that Jesus loved me even when I did not love myself, and I could not love myself because I didn't know how or what love was to forgive the past and who I was then and embrace the present and who I can become by surrendering the future and watch miracles unfold. It was only through Him that I was able to preserve and find the true meaning of what it means to love.

Today, I hope that my story will impact the lives of many who are struggling with the painful effects of addiction. I know He was there to make sure I received everything He has for me by having faith in Him and in His Word. Renewing my mind in God's Word every day has taught me not to hate, hold grudges, be angry, be resentful, or be disobedient. I have learned to forgive those who have wronged me, even when it was painful to do. It shows who I am and that I have His love that abides on the inside of me.

My life experiences have taught me to love and appreciate what God has given me, which are life, liberty, property, and the pursuit of happiness. I never want to take it for granted. I only have one life to live on the face of this planet, so I strive with excellence and perfection to make it my best. Striving for excellence is not a hard thing to do because of Jesus's sacrifice on the cross and the blood that He shed for me and all of us, so that we would not have to go through the fear of being alone. If we only believe in the sacrifice that He paid for our freedom, it makes life a lot easier to deal with and understand, what an amazing grace.

My life experiences are just what I say, a testimony. A testimony of great value to the world because of what Jesus has done for me. He transformed my life at a time when I did not want to continue down that road to destruction. I wanted to change from the way I was living and start living a life worthy of my calling.

I often remind myself that the present is a gift to me and that I must continue to stay focused on where I am going and make the best of my life and live each day with gratitude and thankfulness because tomorrow is not promised although we live without recognizing that it is a very true statement from our heavenly father. I give Jesus thanks every day for letting me be here. I am so grateful for all the wonderful things that I have in my life today. The things that I once took for granted in my younger years to later in life, when I realized what it means to have a roof over my head, a warm bed to sleep in, clean clothes to wear, and food to eat. It is really a blessing to live in the United States of America, where there is plenty. I am here only because of His grace and mercy.

The Father's will is going to be done in my life. I am confident about where I am going and what I am doing. He loves me. I have been redeemed by the blood of the Lamb and the word of my testimony. I can never stop thanking Him for loving me so much that He would not leave me where He found me. He picked me up when I was down in the valley and placed my feet on a solid foundation that is firm and secure in Christ Jesus, and for all he has done for me, I love you, Father God. And if you wonder why I speak so much about God the Father and His Son Jesus, the reason being is because He brought me through a very difficult and horrific time in my life—when I needed a friend, He was there; when I need a savior, He was there. I thank Him for his amazing grace that saved me.

Life in the Beginning

I was born in Columbia, South Carolina. I come from a big family. My big family's circumstances and situations created a drive for survival inside of me, and it is that drive inside me that stands to this day. How we live makes all the differences in our lives. Ruby, South Carolina, is where I grew up. It's where my story begins.

I grew up in a very small rural town. I was born Althea C. Moser Driver, born on June 29, 1956, to the proud parents Carlee and Evelyn Moser. I was born the fifth oldest of thirteen children. I have nine brothers and four sisters. Growing up, we didn't have a lot as kids. My mother worked at the different sewing plants, which was all the work they had where we lived at the time. My father worked wherever he could find work. My parents did as best they could to supply our needs. I grew up like most children who come from big families: I wished for better things.

During my adolescent years, I experienced feelings of inferiority because my parents struggled financially. My mother provided as best she could. Even when she was pregnant, she would go to work to try and make ends so that we could have food to eat. Being poor as a young girl and growing up was very heartfelt. We didn't have a variety of new clothes like other children. It was more or less hand-me-down. When we outgrew the clothes, they were passed down to the next one. Because it was such a big family, my mother basically made the majority of our clothes. I thought I had a normal life growing up, but I guess I didn't. Even in school, I felt like I did not measure up academically to the other kids. I didn't feel I was as smart.

As a young girl, I remember when my dad used to drink and the good times we had with him. He was a lot of fun, especially on weekends, when he would have fish fries on Friday nights. The whole community of family and friends would come over to the party. At that time, I didn't understand the impact that alcohol has on a person's life, the fact that it was a sickness and addiction that eventually takes control. It was after becoming an adult that I understood this crippling addiction. I like my dad better when he was drinking because he was a lot of fun.

I remember one Friday night my dad was having a fish fry. We were all playing in the front yard, and there was a big army helicopter that flew over our house and landed in the big field across the street from our house. The army men came over and partied with us. We had lots of fun with them; they even left some of their canned foods with us. Yes! Those were the kinds of good old days that I remember about my dad, until one day it all changed.

My father had stopped drinking and smoking. He became a totally different dad from the dad of the fish fries. I did not like who my dad had become. He became very strict. The laughter and fun had left; we could not do the things we were used to doing anymore. I did not understand at the time the change that had taken place in his life. He became a preacher. My brothers, sisters, and I became "preacher's kids," also known as PKs. Our lives as preacher's kids changed us dramatically.

From that point on, most of my childhood growing up were spent going to church and school. Those two places were the only two outlets I had. I remember my father working at this plant in Cheraw, South Carolina. The reason I specifically remember is because he took us to a Christmas party there one year. We had fun, and we got lots of toys. We got the chance to meet Santa Claus. It was exciting and fun! I think I might have been seven or eight years old at the time.

Then there was the next Christmas I remember when me and my baby sister got big colored walking doll babies, and my two older sisters got clothes, my brothers got toys, cowboy hats, and guns, and my older brothers got bicycles. We couldn't wait to tear into our Christmas presents under the tree. That was the last Christmas as a child that I remember my family having. It was because of our religion that we didn't celebrate Christmas anymore. It was also the last job I remember my father having.

In our household, there were very strict guidelines. We were not allowed to wear pants, short dresses, or makeup of any kind because we were told that it was a sin before God and this was the way of the world. You were not a saved person if you did such things and you would burn in hell for doing it. We feared our father; he instilled it in us. There were times when my father was abusive. We didn't understand him or his behavior, so we were always in fear of him, especially the girls. It started with my oldest sister, and it continued until we all left home.

My mother was afraid of my father. She tried to protect us as best she could. They were times when she wanted to reach out for help, but back then, we didn't have the support and help that we needed. I also believe fear and shame played a major role. She did not know how to go about seeking the help we needed.

My mom was our only security. When she was at home, we felt a little safer, but we were still afraid because we knew tomorrow would come. Tomorrow was when she would have to leave us and go back to work, then pain and suffering would start all over again. We did not participate in after-school activities, although I wanted to because I was gifted in sports. I could only participate when I went to school. My younger brothers were very gifted in sports as well. We had opportunities that went out the window because my father would not allow us to participate in sports.

Today, I look back and remember how gifted and talented we all were as children. It really made me appreciate and accept how wonderfully created we are all made. I remember how I loved playing volleyball it was my favorite sport in which I was very good at. I will never forget the year our ninth-grade class competed against the other homeroom classes, and we won the championship. I was in Mrs. Susan Ann Davis's homeroom class. She was a great teacher! I ended up being the MVP. I also played basketball and table tennis, among many other sports. I also ran track, in which I was number one! Undefeated!

I remember when school let out for the summer. My summers were spent at home taking care of my younger siblings, who would run around barefoot most of time. They would play jump rope, hopscotch, softball, basketball, running track—you name it, we played it! My baby sister and I, as well as all my girl cousins, were tomboys. There was nothing we couldn't do. We were good at what we did, and we had fun playing against each other! There were a lot of us on the Hill, which was a community in the little town of Ruby. Where I lived was known as the Hill.

My two older sisters and brothers graduated, and they left home to begin their new journey in life. We were sad to see them leave, but we knew it was the best for them. As time moved on, we got used to our sisters no longer being there, yet we looked forward to seeing them come back home for visits. We were always glad to see each other. My baby sister and I could not wait to see the beautiful dresses and shoes that my sisters would bring home. We knew they had pretty things, which we loved, and to hear the stories about life in the big cities where they lived. Me and my baby sister often talked about our life after leaving home—what we wanted to do, where we wanted to live, and most of all, what we wanted to be when we grew up.

There were times when my dad would take us to visit our grandparents on my mother's side of the family. We looked forward to visiting them in the big city of Columbia, South Carolina. To us, the big city was exciting compared to growing up in Ruby. Although they lived in the country, my grandparents had a lot of land with chickens, goats, ducks, and dogs. My grandfather loved his animal species. He was such a loving, hardworking man. I miss them dearly often, I have memories of going to visit my grandparents and the excitement of everything as a child growing up.

Ruby, South Carolina, population 373 was a small town; growing up in the South, there wasn't a whole lot to look forward to. Every day was the same. There was nothing new and unusual happening. There was no growth, which is why we were so excited to go to the big city. It was our vacation for the summer, which we didn't get to do often because my dad didn't work much at all. Then eventually, he just quit working, which was not very much support at home for a family as large as ours.

As I mentioned previously, my father became a minister and said that he was to preach the Word of God, so he quit his job. We were living off food stamps and only living off what my mother made from the sewing plants, which was not a whole lot of money at all. Those sewing plants didn't have a lot to offer, and the pay was not that great. Then there was the little money that my father received from the church. That wasn't enough either because the church was basically a family church on my father's side of the family (meaning that the church was filled with mostly family).

There were others who attended the church that were not family, but the tough times were there and so were financial struggle of survival for the family. We did have a few outsiders who lived in the community, but there was no one to ask for help because everyone in Ruby was just as poor as we were, and as far as faith goes, I'm not sure if my parents understood the true meaning of what it meant to have faith or what faith really was. And I say that because of what I was taught and their belief in the Ten Commandments. I do remember that my father, as well as my mother, were firm believers in the Ten Commandments. They taught us as best they could to believe in God. It was a real struggle for my parents.

I didn't come from an inspiring family of writers. My parents were poor and uneducated. They only understood what they were taught, and they grew up in the environment they knew. The main book that was read in our house was the Bible. I can say that I am thankful today to have had a father and a mother in my life. Even though the circumstances and the situations were not always the best, I am grateful! If God had not brought them together, I would not be here to write and share my story with others who may desperately need to hear some encouraging words.

I miss my parents, but I know they are in heaven cheering me on. Although they did not get the chance to witness the author, speaker, and teacher that their daughter has become, they are seeing it from among the great cloud of witnesses that Hebrews 12:1–2 declares.

I am grateful that I have forgiven my father. Forgiveness has enabled me to move forward in life knowing that acceptance is free.

I encourage you to keep believing in yourself! Know that there is a reason and purpose for everything that happens in our lives. I am forever thankful to my Lord and Savior Jesus for the many blessings that He has bestowed upon me.

As the years went by, I eventually graduated and left home to begin my own life. I did not know what to expect out of life. I really wasn't prepared for what life had to offer. I only knew what I had been taught, so I learned the rest of what life had to offer through experience and from others.

In my senior year of high school, I signed up for the army. That changed the way I had grown up in Ruby, South Carolina.

Military

As I previously mentioned at the end of the last chapter, in my senior year of high school, I signed up for the military. I graduated on July 9, 1974. I joined the United States Army, which was a good thing for me because it helped shape me for the world. I know today that knowledge is power. I was stationed at 574 Personnel Headquarters Station in Hanau, Germany. I was a clerk typist. I processed orders for incoming servicemen and women into the company until I was honorably discharged one year later. The discharge was allowed due to sickness and other complications.

While I was in the military, I met my first husband, Reginald Russell York. He was a Specialist Four at the time, and we both worked at the same company. We started dating and became romantically involved with each other. A year later, 1975, we got married in Hanau, Germany. It was a beautiful wedding with friends and coworkers. Shortly after the marriage, the abuse started. He became physically abusive as well as mentally abusive because of the heavy use of alcohol. Sexual discrepancies contributed to his more violent acts of aggression toward me.

Despite the painful abuse from my husband, I got pregnant, and we had a beautiful baby girl. I was filled with joy on one hand, yet on the other hand, I was afraid of him. The abuse was a constant thing that was always present. Part of the abuse was an unfaithfulness that would surprise and challenge how I grew up. I had no idea that Reggie had another lover. This other lover was named Sally. The only way I can describe Miss Sally is that she was petite and sweet, and she had a 'fro kept ever so neat.

It turns out that the Miss Sally I thought was a she was actually a *he*! I couldn't believe it! I first met Sally when I arrived at my permanent duty station. I had no idea that Miss Sally was actually a man, and that he and my husband were lovers.

To be truthful, I didn't know anything about homosexuality at the time because it didn't exist where I came from, or if it did, I didn't know about it. After leaving military life with my husband, Reggie, we moved to Omaha, Nebraska, where he lived. The abuse did not stop once we got to the states, and the drinking escalated along with the abuse. I didn't know where to go or who to turn to for help because domestic violence at that time was not talked about openly as it is today.

My nights grew cold and lonely as I was left to take care of our child by myself for days on end. Unknown to me, it turns out that he was in another relationship. It would be years later that I found out he was cheating on me with another man. I went through so many painful events with this man. The years of 1978 to 1987 were some of the most difficult years I had experienced. My life was comprised of many broken pieces. I had literally separated myself from my family and God due to an ill-fated marriage. I know how this must have hurt my parents being disappointed in the choices that I had made in my life.

These were dark and evil times in my life where I was faced with trials and tribulations from a sexual orientation that I didn't even know existed. My world seemed to be closing in, and the walls of depression were building up around me. My life had been filled with trauma and fear. The only thing that meant anything of importance to me at the time was my baby, and even she could not save me from myself. She was just a sweet, innocent little lamb who didn't have a worry in the world. She did not know what Mommy was going through or experiencing. All she knew was that Momma was there and that she was not alone and loved very much. She was then and still is to this day the apple of my eye—a love gift from my heavenly Father. Thank you, Daddy, for such a wonderful gift! I certainly wasn't thinking of Jesus being a part of my life because I was not in that type of mind-set. The sense of failure and embarrassment of not being good enough was devastating to me.

I didn't know the things about the Bible then like I know today. It was when I left home after graduating from high school that my journey began. Now that I know that the most important relationship we can have is one with Jesus, it has open my eyes to see life in a whole different perspective because we need to know and understand how God sees us. Since becoming a Christian and a believer in Christ Jesus, I have been strengthened because He says we are His workmanship and His masterpieces. Each one of us is thoughtfully designed by the Creator for His purpose that we may give Him the glory (Ephesians 2:10).

Chapter 1
The Addiction

Blood is gushing everywhere. I'm holding my hands around my neck, trying to apply the right amount of pressure so I can live. At that time, I wasn't thinking about where I was at and what I was doing that caused this all to happen. I just wanted to live. I was afraid that I was going to die although I didn't feel like my life was worth saving because of my battle with the addiction of drugs and alcohol. I do remember asking Jesus to save me as the nurses and doctors rush to help me. I had been stabbed on the side of my neck very close to my jugular vein with a nine-inch chef knife while in a dope house, smoking crack cocaine. This was one of many times and experiences when I know now that it was Jesus who saved me while on the road to self-destruction.

Hello. My name is Althea Driver. Eighteen years ago I was addicted to drugs and alcohol. In my story, I share some of the untold events that happened to me personally, as I experienced over twenty years lost in the wilderness of that dark and evil world of addiction. It truly amazes me now that this day has come, and I am writing my life story of being homeless. Story of being addicted to drugs and alcohol and what a devastating impact that it had on my life. But to see the outcome of it all and how far I have come since my life-changing transformation is nothing short of a miracle. It was years before I got to this place and time in my life. When you are an addict, you are very much in need of help; it's a strong, intense battle with the mind.

You are dealing with all kinds of thoughts that's taking control over your mind making you want more and more because of the way it makes you feel. No matter if it was but only a thirty-second-high, that's the way it's designed to keep you coming back for more; in other words that's the nature of the drug crack cocaine. The need and want to get what makes you feel good.

I would find myself in places I had never been before, but I knew what I was looking for was there. Being an addict, you don't meet strangers; you meet those who do what you are doing. Even if it's your first time meeting, you are looking for your next fix. And that is all that matters at the time. It's not a social visit to get to know you better; it's to get to know where I can get it.

The world of evil addictions such as drugs and alcohol is nothing but a death trap. It's a slow walking death because we find ourselves dependent upon it. It can be a quick death as well. I went through some horrible situations where I had no other choice but to deal with it. There are many hardships when you are entering that way of living, not knowing what each day will bring. There were times when I would get so high that I feared my own self. I thought that I was in control, but it let me know that I was not the boss. I did what the boss wanted, and that was to go and get my next fix because by flesh, the body, needed to feel good. I was not afraid to go any-where. Crack makes you very bold, and so you go where it takes you.

Because you are always figuring out how you can get more. Not that it is always a good idea, but that's the way it delivers, and taking risk and chances you do not mind doing. You have no fear. It makes you rob, steal, and even kill to get your next high or fix. I don't think you realize you have signed your on-death certificate when you choose to go that way. I am so grateful that I never came to the cross-roads where I want to end my life or kill myself.

I know that I would not have normally gone to some of the places I went or done the things that I did, had I not been on crack cocaine. Because when you are an addict, all you want is to keep your habit going and you will do whatever it takes to get you there. Talk about boldness! It does not have no favorites, nor does it discriminate.

I will never forget how painful it was for me I was crying out because I didn't know what I was going to do. I was getting caught up in my addiction. My daughter was with me, and I was trying my best to keep it hidden from her as much as I possibly could. And to this day, I asked why I let myself go that way. Because it cost me everything although it's my past, I cannot change what has happened. Because it's just that, my past, and I will not let it define who I am today! I knew I had to do something and do it quick because time was running out for me, and I had to get my daughter to a safe place or I would end up losing her to the system, and I was not going to let that happen.

And so I called and ask my parents if I could bring her home. It was painful for me to have to face this mountain of knowing that I was going to be separated from my daughter. We were very close at that time, and I was all that she had. Her father and I had been separated for years; later, we divorced, and that was the end of that part of my life.

I took her home and started trying to pick up the pieces of my life and put them back together again. Which was not as easy as I thought it would be. There were still obstacles in the road that I was not prepared for and could not handle.

I started out trying to be undercover with it, but how many drug addicts today know that being an addict is not something you can do, and be undercover with it because it does not discriminate? It doesn't care who you are. It will eventually destroy your life if you choose to go there. I know, because I was there. As for me and my world, it was turned upside down, inside out; it was completely inverted. Everything about what I was doing to myself had almost destroyed me and my life.

During those years that I was dependent upon this drug, I became homeless and started dwelling in that type of environment. I had begun to experience that dark side of what it was like to be on drugs. For years, the addiction became more and more overwhelming in my life. Imagine waking up every day to a life of nowhere to go and nothing to do but try and survive. It became a way of life. The reality of being homeless, was a real game changer as if I had lost a part of me somewhere. Sleeping outside is not like you are in the garden of Eden. I never thought I would go through this, but I did. First of all, I never thought the day would come when sleeping outdoors would become a way of life. It was mind-altering knowing that your lifestyle has changed, causing a numbing effect. It truly was an awakening to the real world of being an addict—addicted to the real world of drugs, alcohol, and homelessness. It was a totally different world that's not healthy for any human being—the effects it has on the mind and body and the things you put yourself through. The world of drugs, alcohol, and homelessness is real, and then you began to see and realize that it is real. After having an experience, I learned that it is a dangerous world for anyone who lives that lifestyle, especially being a woman. I think what helped me the most was the homeless people themselves and the friend I met on my way into this addictive lifestyle. Sleeping outside was a learning experience for me. Meeting people from all walks of life, trying to survive, people just like me and you who at one time had a life, family, a home, a job to get up and go to, and friends to share with, and then one day, the reality of finding themselves in a place of homelessness where the streets had become a way of life and survival.

I began to experience the legality of being in and out of jail. After a while, I started becoming a regular, because the more I stayed out there, the more I would find myself in and out of jail. I was becoming more and more involved in my addictions. I would have no place to stay when I got out, so I would sleep wherever I could. At this time, I didn't have the friends whom I used to have because of the lifestyle that I had chosen to live, and so I had no one whom I could go to for help. So sleeping outside became a way of life for me. I think what helped me to not be so afraid in the beginning of my exodus is because I did not show it and I didn't look the part. I had met someone that made me feel good about being where I was at the time. His name was Piedmont Joe. We became friends. He shared a lot with me about street life because that was the life he lived. He was well known on Ponce de Leon, and this is where I first met Joe. As we got to know each other, I felt safe around him, beginning to feel like I could trust him. And he showed me that I could because he recognized that street life was not where I had come from. I was fortunate to have meet someone like Piedmont Joe because he was different. You don't find too many good people in the streets that's surreal and down to earth, honest with themselves toward you, but Joe was, and he showed me that as we shared our friendship.

As the friendship developed, we became very close, making it known to all his friends and the people of the streets that I was his friend, and so that made life better for me because I was very distraught because I was going through a difficult time in my life as well, and to meet someone like Joe that I could talk with made life a little bit easier for me. Joe was a man of strength for me because I was new to the world of homelessness. As time went on, I found myself becoming one of them, learning how to survive and finding out what it was like to live outside day and night. For years, I kept up my image of not looking like I was homeless. I kept myself together. It wasn't always the easiest things to do, I had lost out on the jobs that I had, but I still maintained a sane mind. I still looked like someone who was going somewhere that didn't look homeless. And then the day came when Joe became sick. I didn't know that he had a history of seizures, and as time went on, they began to come more and more regular. When he first started having them, they were not severe— nothing the doctors couldn't take care of. But as time progressed, they became more and more frequent, like four or five times a day. The ambulance was always coming and taking him to Grady Memorial Hospital. Then the day came when they took him to the hospital, he never came back, and that was the day my world shattered even more because I had lost my best friend forever. I was glad that I had the chance to meet and share those three plus years with him. It's like I said earlier, I was fortunate to have meet someone like Joe. He was a fun guy to be around, always full of joy and laughter, and had lots of friends in the world he had created for himself. Trying to move beyond the pain of agony and defeat was just another setback for I had lost a friend, my partner. The loss was of great effect to me, and slowly, my world started unraveling, so I did what I thought was best, and that was to medicate myself with drugs and drinking that helped ease the pain of heartache and sorrow because that is what I was truly going through, but as time pass on, I eventually move on with my life, and the memories of Joe were good and happy ones. Although I was still dealing with the effects of drugs, drinking, and homelessness, it wasn't making my life any better. I can see and understand why God sent His only Son into the world to save (sinners) crazy people like me from destruction.

I had become what I was, an addict addicted to drugs and alcohol. I also was a heavy cigarette smoker for over twenty years. I could not see myself without a cigarette. I had to have a cigarette first thing when I would wake up. Every time I drink, I was smoking a cigarette. After having eaten something, I had to have a cigarette. It was cigarette, cigarette, cigarette. I would have cigarette hangovers. I am really amazed at how my health has turned out in spite of everything I've been through.

There were days when depression played a major role. I was sad, lonely, didn't have a friend whom I could go and talk to. My life was wasting away. It was like looking at the sand through an hourglass. So were the days of my life. I hated to see daylight because I didn't want to be seen. I was living in so much darkness and evil that I wished it would stay dark all the time. I went through things that I never thought I would experience. The people, places, and effects that drugs have over your life is unbelievable. You can only imagine if you have never been there.

Sometimes the storms of life come without letup. You are caught up during it, and you don't know where you are going to land. They come without warning, and it not what you were expecting to happen, but we miss the point that we are not in control of these demonic forces that have taken control of our minds. The way we think and act is the controlling power it has over you. The more I did drugs, the worse my life became. I found myself finding shelter wherever I could. My whole world was crashing down, or should I say had crashed all around me. There were days when I longed to go inside just to lie down in a nice, warm bed after days of being up, because I would be so tired from battling the raging war on keeping up my habits unfortunate my bed was outside wherever I could find to sleep.

I was a lost, wandering soul with nowhere to go. I would find shelter some nights in the doorway of businesses when they closed for the evening. Behind empty buildings, abandoned houses, sometime even under bridges. And there underneath and old rusty eigh-teen-wheeler trailer truck was where I had my first encounter with the destroyer and my God! It was years later in my life that I was able to see and understand what I had experience and went through under that old truck at that time. I didn't get the revelation or under-standing until I had been delivered out of the storm.

This pattern of my life continued for years. I disconnected from my family because of who I had become. I didn't want them to know that my life had taken a turn for the worse. I had gotten so deep into my addiction that I could only pray and ask God to please help me. Because I knew I was in over my head, and only He could deliver me.

While I was going through the storms of life, five years later, I was in a relationship with my then boyfriend Darnell, who later died of lung cancer in 2003. We had met while living on the streets. We became fond of each other and started sharing with each other our life story. We develop a relationship, and our lives together started becoming of interest to each other. When I first meet Darnell, he had just gotten out of prison. He was a man of great values and character. Even though we were both struggling with the addiction that we were dealing with, in so many ways, our lives were forever changed, trying to put the pieces back together. We were there for each other, and there were times when we had breaks. In the midst of our storms, we both eventually got ourselves a job while being on the streets, and I was so happy, not to mention how proud I was of myself and Darnell as well because things had begun looking up for the two of us, and we were able to get off the streets. At that time, we had been on the streets for over ten years, and things were finally changing for the better. I went to the VA and got involved in the comprehensive work therapy program (CTW), and I was accepted. Then Darnell got a job. He work for a great company that did roofing and canopy for different business. We had a good relationship because of where we were at and what we were experiencing at the time. Before his death, we were staying in a hotel both working now currently. So things started looking up for us. I remember my mother and my uncle came to Atlanta to visit. That was a moment in time I will never forget because I had just started working at the VA hospital. It was a surprise visit that my mother and uncle came by to visit us. And I was very happy to see my mom and uncle Leon. Most of all, she got the chance to meet Darnell, considering everything that has happen, leading up to this time and place. I am glad that they got the chance and opportunity to meet him. He was a wonderful person to know. Although we had obstacles, we overcame them, and today, I am grateful.

I never talked to my mother about my past at the time they visited us, because the visit was a short weekend, and they were passing through to visit someone my uncle Leon knew in Georgia at the time. Although I was glad to see them both, especially my mom. I had not seen my mom since I took my daughter home. It had been at least ten years. After that visit, it was like I had dropped off the face of the planet, never to be seen or heard from again. At the time, I was in the CWT Comprehensive Work Therapy Program for veterans. It was a two-year program. I was place in the Sterile Processing Department, and I worked there for two years.

After that, I got a permanent job working on the fifth-floor mental health service line. I lost my job at the VA hospital, and I was very hurt behind the way I was terminated from my job. I wasn't given any warning that I was going to be fired. I was on a one-year probationary period, and I was fired on their part. My job performance was not the problem; it was the environment that I worked around, and even though I fought for my job, it did not help because their minds were already made up that I was to be replaced.

And because of the loss of my job, with nowhere to go at that time and staying in a hotel room paying weekly, we didn't have money saved up to continue paying weekly rent until we could get ahead with work. We both ended up losing our jobs and could no longer stay there. We ending up coming back to the streets, and that was a big setback for me. The battle of addiction started raging again in my life. I was hurt, angry, and devastated behind losing my job. Because I had worked my way up to that place and time, where I was now in a permanent position or so I thought.

I was not expecting for things to turn out the way they did. It was very upsetting, because I had worked very hard at overcoming the many obstacles that I was being faced with, and to get a job after years of being homeless was a blessing beyond anything I could comprehend at the time; I was so grateful. We found ourselves back in the place in which we had once came out of experiencing: that dark and evil side of destruction and homelessness.

I totally disconnected from family and friends because of my anger and hostility toward the people who had hurt me the most. I was dealing with my emotions physically and mentally. The war of addiction was a raging battle, and there was no peace or comfort in sight. And things did not change until the transformation some twenty years later. Most of all, I didn't want my family to find me because they would have wanted me to come home, and I knew that was the last place I wanted to go.

It would not have been a good decision for me to make at that time. I knew the healing process would have taking a long time, or maybe it would not have been a healing the way I should have. There were times when people would come and share with me, giving me hope and encouragement. I did not have a support system at that time because of my addiction. I wasn't looking for one or trying to find help. I was into my own world and wanted to do things my way.

There were near-death experiences several times during my addiction that was catastrophic and the intent was to be disastrous. I was hit by a car; I did not know what happened at the time because it all happened so fast. I didn't see or feel anything. All I remember was sitting up looking around at where I was at. When I sat up, I remember I was straight on the double yellow lines in the street. I was very much aware of where I was at; I just didn't know how I got there until I was told about what happened. I did not feel any pain or have any broken bones after being hit by this car at a high rate of speed, landing in the middle of the street, lying straight on the double yellow lines, as if someone had caught me and lain me down. When I should have been a bloody mess, there was no blood shed that day. There were no broken bones, yet through it all, I was able to get up and walk to the other side of the street as if nothing had happened.

When every bone in my body should have been broken upon impact. All I know is that it was a miracle from God that He had his loving arms wrapped around me. I can see and say that today because of who I am as a believer in Christ Jesus. I reached back behind me, got my wig, put it on, got up, went to the sidewalk, and sat down. Now that's amazing, to have a mind and be able to get up after being hit by a car and walk across the street and sit down as if nothing has happened. That is truly amazing grace.

I don't know how long l had been lying there, but all I know is that when I rose up, the ambulance and police were there, and they asked me if I were okay. I said yes. About that time, the car that hit me came back. It was a black car, and from the impact of my being hit, it was unbelievable. The front windshield showed where I had gone into it from being hit by the car in which there were no way I should have survived. At the time of the accident, I was on a mission to get some drugs, and I was distracted by others. They were calling me from across the street, motioning for me to come with them.

I didn't see any of this coming, because I wasn't paying attention when I proceeded to cross the street to go with them. I now know why I was not hurt at all when this car hit me, in which I was not supposed to have survived. From this car that hit me, I was supposed to have been killed on impact, is what I was told the next day. At the time, I wasn't looking at what had happened to me, because my mind was on getting what I wanted, and that was the drugs. I did not realize the impact of being hit by this car. After several days had past, I was walking up that same street and there was an elderly man sitting on his front porch as I was passing by. He called me I was surprised that he remembered me, and these are the words he told me he said you are not supposed to be here. He said you need to thank your Jesus, because I seen everything and he told me the story and to see you get up I knew it had to be a God in heaven the Angels caught you and laid you down.

I didn't realize that Jesus had just saved my life from being taken by blocking the devil from destroying me, simply because I was not in that spiritual mind frame of recognizing the love, mercy, and favor that He has bestowed upon me, even when I had not accepted and made him my Lord and Savior. I could have died on impact not having made Jesus the Lord and Savior of my life.

I am thankful and blessed to be here today, all because He has a plan and purpose for my life and to give me another chance to recognize how much he loves us. Even when we are not being his faithful servants. I am so grateful for all the times He has protected me and kept me wrapped in his loving arms. I will never know the disasters that were waiting for me that I never had to experience, all because He was there to make sure I didn't go through them. Only what I was to go through is what I experienced. I am so blessed and honored to be here; until I cannot express my gratitude enough, there is just not enough words to express His love and mercy that He showers upon us. Even when we don't recognize it.

I remember one night I was out looking for drugs, and I was attacked by this man who came up and was trying to rob me. He started choking me. And at that time, I saw my whole life flashing before my very eyes. I didn't realize I had passed out from being almost choked to death. All I knew was that when I came back there was a man standing over me, pulling on me and shaking me, saying, "Wake up, wake up." At that time when I came around, and was aware of my surroundings, I saw this person walking away with his back to me. I never looked at nor saw his face. I got up off the ground and left the area. I never knew who that man was who saved my life, but I thank God for him. Again, I believe that was an angel who came to my rescue.

There was another time when I was stabbed in my neck very close to my jugular vein with a nine-inch chef knife. I was in a dope house smoking when from behind I was struck. When I was told to look out, it was too late. My block wasn't quick enough, but my Lord and Savior stepped in and blocked for me, even though I was told that I would never walk again, when I was inside the ambulance after being asked a series of questions to make sure I was alert. I let them know although the stabbing was detrimental at the time I was a sinner being saved by grace, and that I would walk again because I believed in Jesus.

They took me to the hospital. They had to immediately do surgery to stop the bleeding. The stabbing was so close to my jugular vein that the doctors told me that if I had tilted my neck in any direction at the time of the stabbing I would not have live to tell the story. It's only by the grace of God that I am here today. I thank God for the doctors and their help. They had to immediately begin the process of cleaning my system out so that they could began the surgery. Everything turned out for the better. I was released from the hospital a couple of days later, thankful to be alive.

Knowing I am at the mercy of my Lord and Savior Jesus, because had it not been for the Lord on my side, I would not be here today to write my story. I am so grateful for his love. I was once crossing the street, and a car ran over both my feet, knocking me backward in the street again. There were no bones broken or crushed bones in my feet or legs. I got up and continued to walk. Everything that's happened to me was meant for deadly impact. I was not supposed to survive. But Jesus loved me so much that He would not give Satan the victory he was trying to proclaim. I am here today only because of God's gracious favor and the prayers of my parents and others.

I know that when you live a life of drugs and alcohol your body is not healthy; it is slowly deteriorating or, should I say, dying from what we are putting in it. Your health is at a high-risk factor, and I knew that I had put myself and my health at risk not one time but many times, not knowing what I had contracted over the years. Because I was not going to the doctors for checkups on my health. If there were any illnesses, I didn't know it. I thank God He did not let them continue to linger in my body. Today I am in the best of health. When I go see my doctor for routine checkups, which I do faithfully, she lets me know the outcome. My doctor shows great interest and concern in my well-being when it comes to my health. She is very encouraging and supportive of my life-changing transformation.

I give thanks to God for his grace and favor upon my life, and the doctors as well. I think doctors are a great asset to the human population. Dr. Matthews was very supportive of me when my husband went home to be with the Lord. And I was very grateful for her being there for me at a time when I needed her. She has proven to be very supportive of the veterans who needed assistance. She understands that we all come from different walks of life and from different corners of the globe. I am grateful to have her as my doctor "A Super Great Doctor."

I was not exempt from nothing because of the lifestyle that I was living at the time. When you are addicted to drugs, you never get enough, which was the case with me, and you want more and more trying to get that first high you experienced when you first tried the drug. It's a never-ending battle; it's like chasing the wind, knowing that you will never catch it or see it.

So it is with drugs; you never get enough. It's like the saying in Alcohol Anonymous (AA), "One is too many, and a thousand is never enough!" Before the change of mind took place and the need for help my world had and was spiraling out of control, I didn't have a life. I was making a lot of foolish turns and mistakes in my life. I really didn't know how dangerously I was living, not realizing that at any moment my life could be gone because of what I was doing and where I was at. Sleeping outside was dangerous, even though I was in a relationship at the time.

There were times when I stayed outside: spring, summer, fall, and winter. It had become a way of life, and at one point and time, I was beginning to accept the thought that this is the way it will be because I had wasted a lot of years, and time had just passed me right on by without warning and nothing to show my life. There were times when I wanted to give up, and there were times when I was determined to change the way I was living. I was constantly battling and dealing with the thoughts and mixed emotions that were racing through my mind. It was very confusing and complicated at times.

My lowest point was when anger and depression would over-power me with the thoughts of giving up: "You will never have anything in life," "You are an addict," and so there was constant reminder of no hope at all. I did not know who I was anymore or what I wanted to do with my life. All I lived for each day was trying to keep up the habit that I had become accustomed to. A desperate person full of pain and misery was becoming insane. But because of my addiction, I had to go support my habit by asking for money. There were times when people would give to me because they felt sorry for me. The fact that I was in a wheelchair for almost two years made it much more accessible to get money. The cause for my being in the wheelchair was because I had jumped off a very high wall, not realizing how high the wall was and crushed my ankle bone, and the effect of the fall was devastating and very painful because I was high on drugs. I did not go and have my ankle taken care of at the time, so I was unable to walk.

That wheelchair was a good thing and a bad thing. The good thing is that it gave me relief from having to try and walk on those crutches. I was much more comfortable and at peace. It gave way to me having money all the time, and because I was in a wheelchair, people would give to me because of my situation and the fact that I was a woman and homeless. I then started taking advantage of my situation and used it to support my habit. Some days I would be blessed more than others, but because of my being an addict, I focused on making sure I had money all the time to support my habit, which is what we do. The wheelchair was a great asset to me at the time. The bad thing is.

I would go for days smoking and drinking, always made sure I kept me cigarettes, liquor, beer so that when I would smoke my crack cocaine, I would chase it down with my liquor. Which would even out the rush from the crack, and the crack would keep me from getting drunk so that I could stay alert and would not get drunk; that way, I could continue to drink as long as I had some crack to knock up the high from alcohol. Most of the time, there were always someone to push me around in my wheelchair when I did not feel like pushing myself. By the way, it was one of those manual ones wherein you had to push yourself.

When you are an addict and you out there around others, you have company all the time; in my situation, it was to my advantage. There were times when I would run myself to death smoking crack, staying up all night, living in the dope house, and not to mention again, as I stated earlier, almost lost my life there.

The wheelchair became my greatest asset because it kept me supplied with money to support my habit. I remember people from all walks of life would come up to me and give, and some would come and share the love of Jesus, which I always had a humbling heart effect to hear. It was just something about hearing the love of Jesus; it always made me humble. I knew that it was the right thing to do and what they were telling me was so true. I always accepted it with an open heart. I guess that was God's way of letting me know that He loved me regardless of where I was at or how deep down in the valley of darkness I was. He was there with me, and He didn't take His hands off me. Thank you, Jesus, for your mercy and gracious favor.

There were times when I would be asking for money, in the Publix Grocery Store parking lot, and I met this Jewish man I didn't know at the time if he was a Jewish Rabbi or not but I would ask for money to get food and he would go back to his car and return with a plastic sandwich bags filled with paper money, silver dollars, and coins in the amounts of $400.00 to $500.00. This happened on several occasion. I guess it just happened that I was in the right place at the right time. I would then go and get me a room so that I could be at peace when I go get my drugs. That way, I didn't have to be bother with anyone. I was always being watched, and people would think or just assume that I had money because I was in the wheelchair and was always coming from the boulevard.

I would constantly be going back and forth to the boulevard. And during this time, I lived in midtown on the streets of Ponce de Leon, where there were all types of businesses. And on Ponce de Leon there were also a place where the Homeless men would come to try and get work for the day. They called it the "catch out corner" across from what was once known as City Hall East. Today it's known as Ponce City Market with many different diverse shops and restaurants. And so they would see me. I was well-known on the streets in midtown, and when they would see me coming down, they would come over and push me up the hill to the boulevard so I could get my crack, because they would get some too.

I was going so regular that when they would see me coming, they would come across the street and wait for me and then proceed to push me up the hill to go get my medicine, as we call it, which was where you could go and get just about anything you wanted, and so that was where I spent a lot of time, not to mention the money that I would get and donations for my work. Midtown was a place that lots of homeless people would come to and hang out. I think a lot of them felt safe and secure mainly, because of Ponce de Leon. The street became known for its variety of businesses, and so it attracted all types of people especially the homeless.

It was a haven for homeless people at one time. Because they could panhandle and get money to supply their needs. There were also places on Ponce de Leon that would feed the homeless like the churches and the open-door community center called 910, where the homeless would go to be fed, to take baths, and to get clean clothes to put on. A lot of them use 910 as a place to receive their mail because they did not have a residence because of addiction to drugs. It had become a way of life for many.

Well, 910 was a place that catered to the needs of the homeless. It was a place of restoration for many in need of a place to stay. Or just come and rest from having a long and weary day. It attracted all types of people who needed help. For years, it catered to the needs of homeless people in assistance. Today, it no longer remains on Ponce de Leon. Like so many other places that catered to the needs of the homeless have been phased out, so has the open-door community once called 910 has also left the area, and so has the homeless.

Because change has taken place, I have seen a lot of changes take place since I left the streets eighteen years ago from that life of addiction that was at one time destroying my life. I am so glad that day came when I woke up to the realization that the light had finally came through the darkness, and I was being given the chance to realize there is hope after all, and thanking Jesus for giving me the willpower to overcome. There were many trials and tribulations, but

He made it all possible for me that I would be able to move forward with a made-up mind that wanted to change.

I have seen and heard of a lot of people that I was out there with overdosing and having heart attacks because they just did not know the dangers of what they were doing and getting themselves involved with. I learned the hard way that in the end it was not worth destroying what God has created and instilled within us. To have life and a mind to live is so precious. There is no greater gift to have than life itself, and the evil of this life is not worth losing your God-given identity of who you are, and everything that you were created to be for something that will never benefit or help you in your life time here on earth. Because time is life.

I had become who I was: a sick, mentally depressed, oppressed addict tired of being sick and tired, and realized one day that I needed help because it had come to that point in time where I wanted to change. I didn't know Jesus like I know him today, but at that time, I prayed to Him, asking him to please help me, I wanted to change. The way I was living during the time, I was going through this painful part of life that was tearing away at my whole soul, mind, and body with very excruciating and intense pain. There were people who were good to us in midtown. They would often come out and bring us food and clothing. They would come and share the Word of God with us, and would even give us money.

I remember we would always gather every morning up under the trees at the liquor store called Green Liquor Store. On Ponce waiting for it to open so we could get our medical help or, as some of us would say, our breakfast, so that we could start our grueling day of survival, and so we would meet people as they would come to the store to buy. Also, we would panhandle asking customers for money, especially the painters and construction workers, because they drink and for the most part would buy for us, as well as give us money, and some of them were addicts as well.

And then there were people who would come and share with us to just show love and kindness, I guess knowing that we were homeless and wanted to help. There was a gentlemen we called the Money Man, because every week, sometimes twice or thrice during the week. He would come to Green's drive around and under the trees, where we would be hanging out, and would give us money. He became a regular at doing this, so we started calling him the Money Man. We had a name for everything, even got familiar with the fancy car he would be driving. He would give to all of us who were there. Because most of us were regulars.

This is where everyone would meet each morning, waiting for the liquor store to open, and that way, we would know everyone was alive and nothing bad had happened to anyone. We would have to leave from the place of businesses where we would sleep, whether we felt like it or not at the time. In which we had no choice in the matter because people were coming into their businesses, and they did not want to see you sleeping in front of the store. Most of us were suffering from hangovers and needed a drink to get the shakes off and start feeling better. This was the thing for addicts, because that was the only way we could function. Food was not an option. We were too sick to eat food that early in the morning; the drugs and the alcohol were our breakfast. It helped us get our day started. People were good to us when I was out there, especially during the holidays, like Thanksgiving, Christmas, and the New Year that was coming in. There were lots of love being shown along with gratitude and thankful hearts.

In closing this chapter, I want to show love and gratitude by recognizing and giving a big shout-out to some very special women at Green Liquor Store, on Ponce de Leon in midtown Atlanta. They were there for me as I transformed back from my journey of addiction into the new life that God created me to live and have. The doors were once again open, and I was welcome to come back into the establishment with open arms of love and gratitude. But upon returning, my life was forever changed because I had become a new and living creation in Christ Jesus. So to each one of you, I want to share my love and gratitude toward you.

To Claire Smith Iverson, thank you for being there and a friend who listen to me when I needed someone to talk to. How can I begin to explain how much I appreciate the love, compassion, and care that you shared with me throughout those moments when I was in your presence. To know that you even cared meant a lot to me because I didn't realize at the time that you, being a woman, were looking at my situation differently as enough to show me that "hey, I under-stand and I care!" Thank you for believing in me, and most impor-tantly, thank you for the countless times of encouragement that you poured into me to write this book. To share my story with others, it's a great feeling to sit here and share with you the impact that you have made in my life, showing the love to a woman whose life was shattered from the painful effects of drugs, alcohol, and homeless-ness—the downtrodden you love in so many ways. By reaching out and opening the doors to a place that I was at one time forbidden to come anymore, not to purchase the product itself but to share the transformation that has taken place in my life. Today as I walk in the doors of Green's Liquor Store, I come with joy and thanksgiving to share the love that I feel within the life-changing experience, most importantly blessed to be here. Knowing that my life has been forever changed because of people like you who have given me hope and encouragement to believe in myself, has strengthened me to know that I am somebody in this world today and, most of all, forever a child of the Most High God. Thank you for being a friend.

To Mrs. Barbara Haley, from a sister to a sister, I salute you with love, joy, and thankfulness, thanking you for the love and support that you have shown toward me on the journey called life. Thanking you for being a friend when I needed a friend, because you met me at a time when I was at my lowest, which were very dark and evil times in my life. You seen the struggles and challenges I faced each day, not knowing if I would survive, but through it all and by God's grace and mercy, I overcame. Thanks for all your words of wisdom and comfort at a time when I needed them. The support of this transformation back your being there for me has made me strong, given me great confidence in myself regardless of my past. It's people like you who reach out to those that need love, hope, faith, and encouragement to believe in themselves again. And that is what you showed as a big sister and a friend. I just want to say you will never know how blessed and grateful I am to have known you. Thank you for believing in me, and thank you for being a friend.

To Rhonda Wilson, the sister that tells it like it is with no cut on it. You know I love you and loved you even before I met you. Because I knew we would meet one day (smile). I just want to thank you for the tough support that you showed and shared with me on the journey of addiction. The path that I chose was not a clear one at the time, but I learned that the choices we sometimes make in life can be devastating, which was the case in my life.

Everything that I experienced on my journey back was a lesson well learned. And I am thankful to God for having put people like you in my path as I travel this road call life. You have shown me that no matter what we face in life we can make it better if we keep trying and don't give up. When I was in my world of addiction, I watch women like You, Claire, and Mrs. Barbara every day make your way to work doing positive things with your life. And I would say to myself one day I am going to have that lifestyle again. I didn't know when the change would take place, but the thought of it was instilled in the back of my mind. At that time in my life, I was going through the addiction process of being an addict, and so I chose to work for something that would one day totally destroy me if I didn't change and seek the help that was desperately needed.

Well, my sister, I want you to know that I didn't give up, although there were times when my world seemed hopeless depression was real, but I was determined to continue this fight until the end, regardless of the situation. It is because of strong women like you who encourage me by showing love and great support as I was going through the ultimate destruction of alcoholism and drug addiction that were trying to kill me what helped me to overcome the many obstacles that I was faced with. Today, my past does not define who I am. I define who I am. God has a purpose and a plan for my life. I want to thank you for being there to see the finished product and, most of all, for being a friend when I needed one.

Chapter 2

The Transformation

Now when I look back on the times in my life and see the person in which I was and how far I have come and grown today, it really amazes me. I know without any doubt in my heart whatsoever that God has favored me through it all. That time I spent out there being homeless and addicted to drugs and alcohol, not knowing what lied ahead was nothing but grace and mercy being extended to me. Because I assure you, with the mind-set that I had, it was only geared toward one thing, and that was to keep my habits supplied. And as I stated in the introduction of this book, I had to go through what I went through because it was inevitable for change at the time of what was taking place in my life. I was in the fire, and I had to come out.

I was so deep in the valley of darkness surrounded by evils until I could not have found my way out at that time if I had wanted to. I did not know my way out, but he came and gave me directions, restored me, and made me whole again. I now realize that I had to go through it to come out restored, refreshed, and, most of all, a new and changed person. A completely changed and transformed life with the mind to live a life of well doing as a believer in Christ Jesus, knowing that he is with us wherever we are. It doesn't matter if we are deep down in the valley or on the highest mountaintop; He is there. He is always with us wherever we go.

The things that I experienced and went through taught me a valuable lesson about just how precious our life on earth is. I thank him for the people who crossed my path each day to encourage me and give me the strength, hope, and inspiration to not give up. Because there were times when I could not and did not see my life being productive again, because of the time wasted and the years that had passed me by.

But little did I know what was in store waiting for me was the change of a lifetime. I had an awakened from God when He opened my eyes to see my ears to hear and my heart to receive what he was showing me that it was time for change. And at that very moment, transformation started taking place. There were such a peace that came over me, and the tears were unstoppable. I asked Jesus to please help me, that I didn't want to keep living this way.

Fear had taken control over my life, to the point it was making me think that if I did not change something bad was going to happen to me. I had already seen things that were beyond my control, the destruction of evil. But then I also felt as if God was there letting me know, "I got you, do not be afraid." And that it was time to close out the chapter in this book because my life was beginning to change forever. I felt such warmth and love of his presence; it was so powerful and humbling. Little did I know what was in store for me; I was searching for a life of peace filled with meaning and purpose.

I know now through my awakening that He knew all I wanted was to change the way I was living. The years of living in that environment were beginning to take a toll on my life, and I realized that I was not getting any younger. I had nothing to show for my existence since crossing over into that world of heartaches, along with a whole lot of hurt, pain, and unforgiveness. It was something that I could not do at the time because of the anger that lingered inside of me, being hurt by so many along the way.

But the time had come, and I had made up my mind that I was no longer going to keep living this way. I was sleeping on some cardboard in front of a barbershop, where there were several businesses, me and several other homeless people. I had gone for days without food. I was weak from the drugs and angry for being led astray. If I must boast, I would rather boast about the things that made and showed me how weak I was, not because I loved myself. Love is something very special to the heart and to have and to share; it's something that makes you a better person. I was in search of many things, but the one thing I needed most was love and compassion.

I was determined to do something about my situation, so that night before I went to sleep, I had told my friend to call the ambulance for me in the morning because I was going to Grady's, which is the hospital, for help. And so they did. The ambulance came along with the police. She knew my name and asked me if I was ready. I said yes, and so they put me in the ambulance and took me to Grady's Memorial Hospital downtown in Atlanta, Georgia. After the transformation, change had begun to take place. I felt different about who I was, and each day, my mind became stronger and stronger.

After being there for several weeks, they were trying to find a rehab facility to send me. I would not tell them that I was a veteran at the time because they would have sent me straight to the VA hospital, and I did not want to go there because I used to work there, and I was ashamed of what I had become. I didn't want the people whom I used to work with to see me, and I wanted to do things my way.

After several attempts to get in different rehabs, it was becoming more and more difficult, because I was in a wheelchair at the time, and most places did not accept wheelchairs at some facilities. Eventually I told them that I was a veteran, and I tell you, when I told them that, in a matter of seconds I was on my way and didn't see the bigger picture, because I was in the storm and only thinking my way and what I wanted instead of letting people help me get to where I was supposed to be. After the addiction of drugs and alcohol started coming to the end of my life, the transformation into the new life began to form and started taking shape.

I went into rehabilitation at the VA medical center in Decatur, Georgia. I started the program, but I did not complete it because I had obstacles in my way, due to fact that I was in a wheelchair and needed assistance with trying to get help with my surgery for the ankle that was broken. I was told that I had to find my own, so I was given a roll of $10 tokens for bus fare to help me seek shelter elsewhere. Currently I was staying at the Salvation Army shelter, which was a part of the VA for veterans.

I had my belongings, and I could not carry them on the bus because of my situation. I felt so disappointed in the system treating me this way and me being a veteran, not to mention the fact that I am female and disabled and they would not assist me in finding shelter. I went back to Grady Hospital, where the surgery was scheduled to take place, and waited overnight so that I could see the social worker the next day and explain what was going on with my situation.

Time was of the essence for me because I need to have my surgery done so that I could start walking again, because I wanted out of that wheelchair, and eventually it happened, but it was a long and exhausting process. This was a part of being tried and tempted along the way because I had made change in my life, and I was determined that I was not going to go back to the life that I once lived of addiction. I continued to press forward despite the temptations. My social worker found me a place to stay leading up to my surgery; it was a rooming house across town in the hood neighborhood called Adamsville.

I was in my wheelchair and had to push myself about two blocks before I could get to the house, and there was a very steep hill I would have to climb before I reached the house. It was very frustrating, and so I did this for about two weeks, not to mention the fact that I began to have problems with some of the tenants that lived there.

I was becoming very unhappy with my situation, so I would go back and forth to the hospital to visit my social worker and let him know what I was being challenged with, and he would assure me that he was working on getting the surgery updated so that I could come in and have it done, and that way, he would be able to find me a place to stay while I was in the hospital recovering from the surgery.

And so everything worked itself out. I was able to go in for my surgery, and after the surgery, I stayed a week in the hospital. My social worker found me a rehab to go to while I was there. I met this nurse named Mary who worked there, and she had a place for people who could not afford to pay for rehab. And currently, I was no longer in the program at the VA.

When Grady released me from the hospital, I went to my new home and started my rehabilitation. Within a couple of months after being there, I started making very good progress. I met a friend whom I knew was homeless who was living there at this place. Marvin was his name, and he helped me regain my strength and confidence.

Each morning, he would go up to the big house and bring back my breakfast because I was not able to walk. My foot was in a cast, and those first six weeks for me was very painful. I was thankful that Marvin was there to help me out. It was a process one day at a time I gradually gained my strength. After eight weeks, I went back and had the cast removed, and they put me in a boot. So I started getting up, walking every morning. Marvin was my trainer. I had to walk from one end of the driveway to the other with my roller about one block, and each day, it got better, and I got stronger and stronger.

After eight weeks of more intense therapy, I went back to the hospital and had my boot removed. I was then walking with a cane, and I could wear my tennis shoes. I was feeling really good about myself and the progress I was making on the road back to recovery. After leaving the facility, I would go back and visit Marvin to see how he was doing. Then one day, when I went to see him, he was no longer there. I was told that he had passed away at the hospital. I was stunned to hear the news. My heart was broken; again, there was another painful moment in my life.

I had known Marvin for many years. He was homeless too, and I know now that it was not by accident that we just happened to be in the same place at the same time. God brought us together to share one last time. I was very grateful for him helping me at a time when I needed help. I was glad that we had crossed each other's paths once again, not knowing that it would be our last. But the moments that we shared were very humbling in the end. I was so glad that we share those specials moments of gratitude, and to let him know that I appreciated his help. Thank you, Jesus, for bringing us back together to help each other with words of encouragement.

While staying at this facility, I had the opportunity and pleasure to meet the woman who owned the care facility: Nurse Mary! She came down and visited me in the little green house, where I was staying with the others. I had the opportunity to meet and talk with her, and in doing so, we established a relationship, which was not by accident either but one that was meant to be. Not knowing that this woman was going to make a big impact in my life.

I spoke with her several times upon my getting ready to leave this place because my time was coming to an end. She was working on lengthening my stay for several more days. During that time, we got to know each other in a very positive way. Before I left, she told me that she had a car that belonged to her son. He was not using it anymore because he was getting a new one. I ended up getting the car. I was so happy, excited, and overjoyed to have a car again. After years of being homeless, the pieces of my life were beginning to come back together again.

And Nurse Mary was just another angel that He had put in my path to share love and to give hope, encouragement, and inspiration along the way. Knowing that there would be many more to come, like my friend Alton, whom I had met not knowing at the time that he was going to be my husband one day. Who at the time was also going through the program at the Salvation Army while I was there. We had classes together, and so we became friends.

After my classes were over, it was like I was pushed out the door with no explanation, and I myself did not know why or for what reason I was being mistreated. They were aware that I had to have surgery on my ankle, but to them, it was as if what mattered most in my life at the time wasn't important to them.

After experiencing the loss of my job when I worked at the VA hospital and then this experience with the drug rehab program that I was in, to me it seemed like the VA had a vendetta against me. I did not understand why this was taking place the way that it did. I was in desperate need of help as a veteran. It was something that I knew I had to accomplish to be able to move on with my life and to meet the goals that I had set to be accomplish. Letting go and moving on, I remember how hurt I was when I got fired from the job I loved and did well. But had not that happened, I would not have what I got today. I was fighting to hold on to something that was not meant to be any longer. God was closing that door so that others could be opened. Today I am living proof that we must realize and understand when it's time to let go and move on to where God is taking us to. The blessings I have in my life today had I not left that place it would not be. I didn't realize that God was rearranging things and that things were happening for a reason because he had taken control of my situation. I had a lot of mixed emotions—hurt, anger, and disappointment—that I was dealing with at the time.

Only God knew and understood the hurt and the pain I was going through at the time; that's why he took control of my situation, because He was quickly moving me ahead, getting me to the place He wanted me to be so that the rest of my journey could be completed. The surgery took place. Mission accomplished. I've learned that when you are in the storm you can't see or understand what's happening with you until the storm is over. I now understand that I was in the storm, but after coming out, I can see clearly now that the rain is gone.

In all my trials and tribulations that I was being faced with through my adversary, the devil, what was meant for evil, God turned around for my good. I was determined to stay grounded no matter how tough the road ahead became. He was showing me that He was there for me, and that was when I knew I was on the right path. To continue knowing that things were going to get better and better for me as long as I kept the faith and believed in myself. Knowing that I can do all things through Christ Jesus who strengthens me (Philippians 4:13).

Chapter 3

Our First Apartment, then the House

AFTER THE TRANSFORMATION, I STARTED connecting with the resources that I was being directed to. I went into a drug rehab program at the VA Medical Center. I met Alton, whom I knew nothing about. It was through classes we shared. After going through my ordeal with the VA, I had the surgery I needed, and was making great progress while going through my healing. I occasionally would run into Alton.

It was like it was always the right time when we would meet. This happened on several occasions, not knowing what was being prepared ahead for me. We eventually ended up getting together. He got us a place to stay. My first apartment. I was so happy, excited, and grateful to God because I had a roof over my head that I could call home, after being homeless for so many years. It was like heaven on earth; so beautiful.

We continued working on establishing ourselves diligently with the VA. Soon I was established with my benefits as well. Things really started shaping up for both of us. We were both excited and happy about the way things were going with our new life.

We got our credit straightened out. We started looking at houses after working on getting our credit repaired. We felt that it was time to start thinking outside the box. And after having conversation with Jesus and asking Him to bless us with a house, our dream came true on July 27, 2010. I signed the papers for our house. It was a moment in time that I will always cherish, I could not believe this was happening after everything I had been through in my life leading up to that day.

The dream house came to life. After moving into our new home on September 7, 2012, we were married. I was very honored to be Mrs. Driver. It was so amazing how all this happened so quickly. It was mind-blowing how everything worked in our favor, and we accomplished that dream, one that I thought would never happen. It did. I never dreamed I would be signing the papers for our home. That was another Aha moment because I was putting my husband in place to be the one to sign off on this house; he was the one who had the credit score. Mine had just begun to take shape. It didn't matter with me who signed; I just wanted the house. I was just surprised that it was me because I knew that I was not ready for this.

But when everything was said and done, I was told through the mortgage company that I was going to be the one to sign for the house. On July 27, 2010, I signed the papers for my first house ever. My husband was happy about it because he wanted me to start establishing myself, and I could not have been happier. I could not believe how it seemed like everything we touched at that time turned to gold. It was happening so fast we had to pinch ourselves to see if this was really happening. We were so excited about our new home we couldn't wait to get our furniture and start the decorating process.

Oh, it was so much fun. We were like two kids with a brand-new toy. I found out a lot about who I was and the gifts and talents that were created in me. The original design that the designer Himself had made was displacing her talents. I never knew all this was breathed into me as a spiritual being. We took our house and turned it into a beautiful home and enjoyed every moment that we shared together. It was unbelievable.

We didn't know and realize how blessed we were. We had no problems with establishing ourselves because God had already done that for us. So our new home was becoming more and more alive every day. I was amazed at how I transformed our home with new furniture, and the things we had from our apartment fit perfectly with the house. After getting set up in our home, we planned a housewarming party and invited friends and family.

It was one month after we moved on September 18, 2010. It was a beautiful, sunny day for our housewarming. Everything turned out just the way we wanted it. We had a good time. My friend Gracie catered the food, and we had lots to offer. It was just a fun-filled day, thanks to friends and family which were just like family although my family wasn't here for my housewarming my other family were. I really didn't expect for things to happen so quickly, but now that I look back at everything that was taking shape with me and Alton, I see life was supposed to be for the very purpose of our every step being ordered of the Lord.

On September 7, 2012, me and Alton were married. Our union was complete. I was Mrs. Althea Driver and was very proud to be his wife. Because God had brought us together, I knew that Alton was the man whom I was to marry. I had a wonderful, loving husband. He was a compassionate and caring man. Everything that we were receiving was a part of where we were going; it was working for our good.

Until that unexpected moment in time when he was diagnosed in March 2013 with stage-4 liver cancer. On April 28, 2013, Alton, my husband, went home to be with the Lord. Oh, what a painful and devastating moment in time that was for me.

My life was changed forever, never to be the same again. It's been six years now, and I must say it's been quite an adjustment of not having his presence around, only the memories to cherish and behold the good times of our life together. I thank God for His grace because it has helped me to overcome the fears of being alone. I was so happy that my family got to know him and be a part of his life. That was so important for me and him that our families accepted our relationship to be with each other.

Today I am at peace because I have embraced the change, remembering the good times we shared and thanking God for letting me be a part of his life. Today I have shared a part of my life story's personal journey with you through it all. I have learned to love and enjoy others, taking nothing for granted because life is so precious. I was so happy that my family had come to spend Thanksgiving with us, and to see the house was just a wonderful Thanksgiving I enjoyed with my family, and they enjoyed their visit with us as well.

They were very proud of me and the progress that I was making in my life from whence I had come was nothing but the miraculous favor of God on my life. From that time moving forward Me, Al, and Bitsy went home for Thanksgiving to be with the family. We all center Thanksgiving around Mom and Dad. My parents were older and could not travel as much due to their health.

Since February 2015, both Mom and Dad have gone home to be with the Lord. I miss those moments when Me, Al, and Bitsy would pack up and head home to Ruby to be with them for the Thanksgiving holidays. Walking through the front door, looking into my mom's big brown eyes and that beautiful smile on her face. Just to see their faces, we were blessed. And then the time came when it was just Me and Bitsy going home to Ruby for the holidays. Al had transitioned home to be with the Lord, but we continued to make the journey each year.

I looked forward to spending the holidays with my family because it gave me peace in the midst of my storm with Al not being with us. This was healing for Me and Bitsy because I know she wondered where her daddy was and why he wasn't coming home anymore. There is a story I want to share about Bitsy and how she became a part of our lives. I am so happy that we rescued Bitsy. She was two months old when we got her the week before Thanksgiving, and she quickly became a part of the family, the love of our lives. She was a joy to have and full of surprises every day, watching her grow up. She was her Daddy's heart.

His love for her was unconditional. She was the apple of his eye, and she knew it. She was crazy about him. Then when the reality set in that he wasn't coming back home anymore, the grief was unbearable. She missed him something terrible when he left the two of us. My baby grieved like she was a human being. I never thought I would experience something like this. She knew something was wrong because she didn't see her daddy's red truck turning into the driveway anymore, not to mention seeing him come in the house. It would bring tears to my eyes to see her this way. I wished at the time that I could have explained to her where daddy was at and she would have understood.

The only thing I knew to do was to love her and let her know that Mommy was there for her. This went on for quite some time. I took her to the doctor, and she explained to me that dogs grieve the loss of their masters. Which helped me to be able to help her and myself get through this together. Even today, after six years, there are times when I believe she still looks forward to seeing her daddy come home, as I watch her emotions. It would be those special moments that I would see in her. I could not let her see me crying, as painful as it was. I had to stay strong for her and give her all my love, knowing that I was all that she had left in this life. And I vowed to my husband that I would always take care of our baby! She is nine years old now, and still looks young very healthy and attractive. She is a pretty girl. We are inseparable. I never knew how loving and special dogs can be. I have learned so much from Bitsy. I am so glad that she became a part of our lives.

Today we both are moving on with our lives and adjusting very well together, with it being just the two of us. I think she has gotten used to it being just me and her now, as if she knows her mommy is there. She's happy, and I am happy to have her as part of my life. I have learned to appreciate all the goodness that has come to me because I know it's meant to be a part of my life, and is something I look forward to. Now I know why Bitsy became a part of our lives, because the day was coming when it was going to only be just the two of us. Only God would know this, and in time, He knew I would see the picture for just what it was meant to be. And I did with gratitude and thankfulness to a loving and wonderful Father.

He brought us through one of the most hurting times of my life, not knowing how it was all going to end, but He did. I had to keep believing and trusting in Him as I continued this journey.

Today, me and Bitsy travel, spend a lot of time together at the park with other dogs. I watch her run and play. She is very active and full of life. She is getting older but has lots of energy, and she looks great. We have many more wonderful years to share onward toward our destiny, taking it one day at a time. I love my baby. She has brought so much joy into my life, and I will always be there for her. Love you, baby girl! The family they were very fond of Bitsy and she knew and look forward to seeing them as well. She was always happy to see them. They would tell Bitsy that she acts more like a human being than a dog (smile).

My parents were very proud of me and the changes that had taken place in my life. They were all surprised to see the accomplishment that I had made and to be a part of the dream that had come to life and now they are in heaven among that great crowd of witnesses cheering their children on for greater greatness and success until we meet again.

Chapter 4
The Family Reunion and the Marriage

IN THIS CHAPTER, I SHARE the homecoming to reunite with my family after years of being missing in action. After spending years of being homeless. When I got to the Salvation Army, after going through the rehab program for veterans and having been clean and sober for almost four months, I made that long awaited phone call to my parents that night. And when the phone rang, my dad answered the phone. I said, "Hi, Dad. This is Althea, your daughter." My dad's response was "Whooooo?" And so I had to give him time to digest this, because I knew it was a big shock to hear from me (smile).

After years of them not knowing where I was at or even if I was still alive to hearing my voice again, I can not imagine what was going through his mind at the time. I do remember hearing my mother screaming and hollering in the background, saying, "Thank You, Jesus!" She must have grabbed the phone from Dad, and her first words were, "When are you coming home?"

I gave them the day that I would be coming home. I felt so much better after having talked with them. The feeling at the time was something I could not explain, because it had been years since I talked with my parents. The next day, the phone lines at the Salvation Army were blowing up. My family was calling me from everywhere. Mom and Dad had told them that I had called, so I guess everyone wanted to see if it was true. When that day arrived, I went home to meet and be with my family whom I had not seen for years. It was a wonderful family reunion.

I will never forget that day when I pulled in at the Greyhound bus station in Columbia, South Carolina. And there they were: my mother, along with my brothers, including my daughter, whom I had not seen since I brought her home to live with my parents. I was excited but nervous all at the same time. But to see their faces meant the world to me, especially my mother's, whom I had longed to see and hug. There were lots of hugs that day.

I spent a month at home with my family. I was really happy to be home and to see my family again, especially my daughter. The little girl whom I once knew had matured into a beautiful and smart young lady. Just to see her brought tears of joy, to actually be looking at her after everything that I have been through. It was the most wonderful day of my life, holding my baby girl again, the one I birth into the world. I often think about the day she was christened in the church we attend when me and her father were together. I will never forget that Sunday morning when we took her before the altar, and the minister held her up in offering back to God. She was dressed so beautifully in a pink and white little dress with lace around the edge with matching white socks and booties. It was a moment of gratitude and thankfulness to my Lord and Savior Jesus Christ for the gift we were giving back and for making that day possible for me to behold the wonders of his glory. There were many days when I wondered how she was doing and what she looked like. I knew each day in her life was bringing changes because she was growing up, and that was a part of her life that I feared for and missed the most because I was not there. But I knew that life for her and me were very different. I had asked Jesus to prepare me for what lay ahead and to take this one day at a time because the healing process had just begun for me.

I adjusted very well and was in good spirits. I was thankful for everything that my parents had done for me. We talked about everything, from what happened to how do you get to that place in your life. I wanted to be as open as I possibly could, because growing up in Ruby and being raised in the country, my parents only understood their world, not the one I had discovered. Where I came from, you didn't have to worry about violence, shootings, and things like I have seen here. There you could leave your doors open when you went to sleep at night and feel comfortable in your house.

Because everybody knew each other and had no fear of anyone walking in without knocking at the front door. They would be in a world of trouble. But then everyone talked so loudly until you could hear them a mile down the road, so you knew who it was. I mean, it was that type of environment that I came from: born and raised in the country, grew up on the farm where my mother and grand-mother raised chickens and hogs. They even planted gardens. My grandmother had the biggest of all, and she would makes us grand-kids help her with her garden. She planted everything. My grand-mother, we called her mother she was my father mother.

I knew there were lots of things they probably wanted to ask me about, and so I was open for that because there had been years of separation from my family. I know there were lots of things they wanted to talk about, and we did share a lot together while I was there for that time and the many times to come. There were some closures to some of the things my parents wanted to know, and I felt better after sharing with them about some of my past. It lifted my spirits even more because they could understand and see things in a different perspective, and it made me feel welcome.

When I went back home the second time to visit my family, I was driving my own car. I remember my mother asking me one morning. We were in the kitchen, sharing breakfast. She asked me did I have a car; at that time, I did not. But I told her that when I come back home again, I would be driving my own car, not realizing that I was speaking and calling that car into existence. And when I went back to visit my family, I was driving my very own car.

From that point in time, everything was changing for the good in my life. I continued to visit home, often taking my husband and Bitsy from then on. My family became very fond of Alton. He was loved by everyone; my parents thought highly of him. Alton was no stranger anywhere he went because people love his personality and character; he was a people person with a very humble spirit and a smile that just won your heart because he always had a smile on his face. He was just a wonderful person to know. I met Alton at the Salvation Army, where we both were in the drug rehabilitation program for veterans.

We shared classes together at the time I was there. After leaving the program, I went on to seek help in getting my surgery on my ankle that I had broken done so that I could walk again. I didn't think I would ever seeing him again, but little did I know, we were crossing paths regularly, and it was as if it was meant to be, not knowing at the time he was going to be the man in my life. I was not looking for anyone to be in a relationship with. My plan was to start a new and refreshed life with just me and Jesus. I wasn't looking for a partner, but it seemed like every time I went downtown, I was running into Alton.

And he was always updating me about his situation and the progress he was making, and I would always tell him how happy I was for him because he had been through a tough battle with drug addiction, struggling to pick up the pieces of his life and starting a new beginning knowing how difficult it was because I myself were dealing with same things. So I went downtown again, and guess who I ran into? You got it, Mr. Alton, and this time, he was telling me the good news about having received his VA benefits. He was so happy, and I was happy for him. Things were beginning to look up for Alton, and seeing that sense of peace and clam that he was expressing, it showed that he was at a very good place in life. I could not have been happier for him. The road that was once rough and jagged were beginning to be smoothed out. We continued to keep in touch. At that time I was dealing with my situation, he had gotten himself a phone and wanted me to have his phone number. I will always remember the call to have lunch with him. He was so excited about the two of us having lunch together, and that time, our transportation was Marta. I met him at the bus stop, and while we were waiting for the bus, he was asking me about the apartments that were there across from the bus stop. So he told me to wait, that he was going to go and see how much the rent was for those apartments.

I did not know that he was going to be getting me a place to stay. He had been up there for quite some time, so he called me and said, "I am coming down to push you back up here so you can sign the lease for your apartment."

I could not believe what was happening. Then he came down and pushed me back up to the office. I signed the lease and got the keys, and we went and looked at the apartment. I was happy that he had done this for me but confused all at the same time. So after everything was taken care of, I told Alton that I could not afford an apartment because I did not have any income coming in at the time, and most of all, that I was not in love with him and so I didn't know how this was going to work out.

But this was what Alton told me. He said this to me: "Althea, all you need right now is structure in your life, and once you get that, you will be able to take it from there. I know you are not in love with me, and I understand that you are not where you want to be financially, but everything is going to work itself out."

He was right. Everything did work itself out. I felt that love and compassion that he shared that day with me. He was truly being a friend, and in this day and time, we need to love and uplift one another. So after getting the apartment and having our talk about this, he took me back down to the rehab, and I got my belongings, which was not a lot. I could carry everything in my lap as he pushed me back up to my new home.

I was at peace, thankful. We then went out to lunch, sharing in laughter having a good time, and he brought me back. I went to my new home, gave the Lord thanks, and I went to sleep on the floor, which had a fresh new carpet. It didn't bother me at all that I did not have a bed to sleep in at the time. I was just so glad to have a place to call home, a place to lay my head and not worry about the fear or danger around me anymore because I was now inside where I felt safe.

Al went back to the Salvation Army and completed the drug rehab program; after completion, he came out to live with me, and our relationship began. We began sharing with each other and getting to know one another. The adjustment of getting to know each other worked itself very well because we were of two different cultures, and I had never share in a relationship with a white guy. It was very interesting to see how this was going to work itself out. I must say it was the best move I ever made. Didn't take long, because our attitude about life and where we had come from where we were going made all the difference in the world.

We were both broken, having suffered a lot of physical and emotional abuse in that world of addiction. We were beginning to put the pieces together very quickly. Each day was a work in progress. We both went through many trials and hardships, but for the most part, our lives had changed for the better. While getting to know each other, I was very excited about the way things were beginning to take shape in our relationship. We were very supportive of each other and working together to make sure our dreams of what we were trying to accomplish together came into being. We both had different doctors and clinics as veterans, but we were successful in getting our benefits started and getting past things in our lives straightened out, like debts that had occur before the addictions took over our lives that carried us in different directions.

Our minds became stronger, and so did our faith, as we shared the Bible, reading each morning before starting our day, not realizing that we were planting seeds of greatness. Thanking Jesus for our new life because it was through Him that we were able to have and enjoy our new apartment, which I always called my little piece of heaven. Because that is exactly what it was. I had come to a place in my life that I could call home. What an exciting moment and time that was. We signed the lease on June 2, 2006, the month that both our birthdays were in Al's Birthday June 8th and My Birthday June 29th. It was truly a dream come true for me, something I never expected to happen so soon. We had both come from a world of destruction and had reached a place in time where we knew it was time for change, not to mention the fact of wanting this change.

I did not know him at the time that he was going through his struggles with drug addiction, and he didn't know me. It was by faith that we were brought into each other's life. We were both searching for peace and tranquility in our lives. We realized the empty void that needed to be filled, and it wasn't in that world of drugs and alcohol that we would find that peace that surpasses all understanding to be delivered from darkness. We keep running in search of the peace of mind that we so desperately needed. And at the right place and time we met, we then knew that this was the change we had been longing for, and to see it taking place in our lives, we recognized and embraced it with open arms. Before things ever developed into being, God had already shown me this relationship long before it happened. But I refuse to accept it because it was not what I wanted in my life at the time. And of course, I questioned Him about this not realizing he knows what's best.

I only wanted to be a friend to Alton and nothing more. But that wasn't the way God saw it. He was bringing into perspective the way he wanted things to be, and I had no control over what was fixing to take place, but it was all for my good. I could not see the picture clearly at the time. Neither did I understand what was going on and why things were to be the way it was going to be. My feelings and emotions were taking over, and I could not see the bigger picture. Not knowing that in time everything would work itself out for the good and I would understand perfectly why He chose Alton to become a part of my life.

And going through the "I don't want this," in the end, I humbly accepted who He had placed in my life with gratitude and thankfulness, because he had opened my eyes to see what I could not see and, most of all, what a loving God we serve. He meets and understands our every need, a God whose thoughts are not like our thoughts. He knows what we are going to say before we say it. He was preparing me for what lies ahead, the real world in which we live.

Chapter 5

Joining WCCI, the Bible School and Graduation, My Testimony on TBN, Women Prison Ministry

JOINING WCCI WAS A LIFE-CHANGING event for us. We joined World Changers Church International in 2007, became members, and graduated from the New Member class, officially becoming World Changers. We knew this was the church for us. Leading up to becoming a part of the church God had already ordered our every step, from the deliverances of our addictions to walking through the doors of World Changers Church International. He prepared our every step. And when we arrived, I received conformation on everything that me and Alton were reading about in the Bible but didn't fully understand some things. He sent us to the place where we could get understanding and revelation about the Bible.

As we began to participate more in our church, we began to grow in the Word of God, and I could see how it was changing both our lives. My husband's whole perspective about the Bible was becoming so real he became more interested in what we were learning and being taught. As time went on, he started beating me out the door for church. He was really seeing the change in both our lives. Because our understanding of how much Jesus loves us started becoming more real and clearer to us. He looked forward to our time together, sharing in the Word. Because we had come to a place where our understanding of the Bible was being enlightened and our minds were being transformed to the ways of Christ.

I remember when me and Alton first moved into our little one-bedroom efficiency apartment. I started thanking Jesus for the blessing of my new home every day, with prayer and thanksgiving, by reading my Bible, and after being taught the importance of reading the Bible every day, I begin to understand the importance of renewing your mind in the Word and how we benefit from spending time in the Word of God.

When we first started our new, transformed life, we had not found a church yet to attend. I had gained weight, so I was looking for a gym in the area. I discovered one called Ladies Only Total Fitness. I liked it at that time because it was what I basically was looking for, so I joined and started meeting other women. It was like one big family. We look forward to meeting and sharing in our workout. I loved the trainers, they were very good. And the workout was just, that a good workout.

So one day, we all were talking about the different ministers that had mega churches, so I asked about Pastor Dollar. Robin, who was my trainer at the time, let me know that she went to his church. I was telling her about how I had heard him on television, and I like the way he was speaking on the Word of God. She then said that if I want to go to church that following Sunday that she would come by and take me. And of course, I was excited about that, so I went with her that Sunday, and I could not wait for Pastor Dollar to come onstage. I was very excited about being there.

I had never been to a church that big before, and even though it was huge, I was more excited about hearing Pastor Dollar. Nothing else mattered at the time. I guess you could say I was hungry for the Word of God. I needed understanding about some of the things that I was reading that I did not understand. After making several visits to this church, it was like my steps had been ordered, and I knew this was the place that I was to go. Every time we went to church, Pastor Dollar was giving us answers to the questions that we could not answer. It was amazing how we were getting revelation and conformation on what we were sharing in our Bible study when we would go to church. We looked forward to church services on Sunday and to Wednesday-night Bible studies.

Not knowing that he was going to be speaking on what we had already shared in our Bible study that morning or the day before. It was amazing. I just could not believe how we were being connected to Jesus the way we were. He was answering all our concerns through this anointed man that He had put before us. It was like when we went to church, He the Holy Spirit was pouring into him every word that He wanted Pastor Dollar to share that day with us so that we could get understanding and closure. It was truly meant for us because He wanted us to get clarity and understanding of what we were reading each day.

That's when I knew without any doubt that this was the place that we were supposed to be because everything was coming together. I was blessed because I received what I was looking for. I could not wait to hear him again and again. Our lives transformed rapidly, and there was a time when the devil would approach my husband with his past life, like he did on occasions when we first moved into our apartment. But he didn't get the victory anymore because our faith and belief in the Bible was anchored strongly in the finished works of Jesus. I was so glad that we had come to the place where we were being taught about the cross and what it represented. On April 9, 2013, I went to World Changers Bible School (WCBS), which offered a two-year associate degree in Christian Studies. It was perfect, just what I needed: more knowledge and understanding about the Bible, which is the true living Word of God.

I must give the credit to my husband for encouraging me to go to the Bible school on campus. I was so excited to know that because I was planning on going back to school, and I had not decided on what I was going to take. I knew I wanted to help others because of my experience with addictions that had almost destroyed my life. So I had thought about becoming a counselor. When people would hear me sharing my story, they would often tell me I would make a great counselor. I knew I had a gift that I could use to help others in so many ways, because I had been delivered from a world of pain and torment. And so I went to the Bible College, and I tell you, it was just an amazing experience for me. I learned so many things about the Word of God until it was just mind-blowing and rejuvenating.

I was raised in the church as a little girl growing up until I graduated from high school and left home, but the things I was taught by my parents were what I understood as truth, and they did too. But as I started growing in my learning from the Bible school, it really opened my understanding up, and I began to see the meaning of the Word, how we must live so that we can be successful in our everyday lives. Everything that I was being taught was what I needed to know. I was grateful for the anointed men and women of World Changers Bible School whom God had put in place to share his message with the class of 2015.

And I was a part of that class, making a mark that can never be erase. It created in me the ability to know that we all have a purpose in this world that we must fulfill on this journey to our destiny. I went on to accomplish that dream, but not without sorrow during my first month of starting class. My husband was diagnosed with stage-4 liver cancer. To hear this devastating news, I felt like I had been sucker-punched in the stomach. It was not what we were looking to hear because our lives had changed for the better, and we were planning and living life one day at a time, never expecting to hear anything like this. I had to drop school so that I could be with my husband because things had changed drastically, and he was more important to me than school was at the time.

After being told by the doctors there was nothing else they could do, for him, it really took some time for everything that was happening to sink in. And seeing what he was going to have to deal with was very heartbreaking at the time. I really had to be strong through it all just for him. My husband was strong willed, and he showed no fear of dying. I know it was because of where God had brought us to and we were knowledgeable of the Word of God. Thanks to his anointed man Pastor Dollar for teaching us the way. His favorite scripture was 2 Corinthians 5:8: to be absent from the body is to be present with the Lord.

After being diagnosed, Alton was given six months to live. We came home from the VA hospital. Two weeks later, he went home to be with the Lord. My life was forever changed in so many ways that I was not prepared for, because I had never experienced the loss of a spouse and having to move forward without him was a numbing, painful, hurting effect that I could not accept and deal with at that time.

I was hurting, and did not know how I was going to do this without his security physically and financially. We had accomplished a lot together in such a short period of time, and to have the responsibility of dealing with everything myself was a very big mountain that I had to climb to overcome, and I was not prepared for this. There were moments of fear and doubt. I had never owned a home before, but my husband played a major role in showing me the value of homeownership because he had experience in homeownership and knew what it consists of, so he was teaching and showing me how to take care and appreciate all the blessings that we had received. Not knowing that I was coming to the crossroads in my life where I was going to have to continue this journey without him.

He was going to be leaving me, and so I was being prepared for what was ahead, not realizing it at the time. I will not say this part of my life that I experienced was not painful, hurting, and, most of all, traumatizing, because it was, and had not it been for His gracious favor on my life surrounded by caring family and friends, I don't know what I would have done. I know from the beginning of our relationship we had made the right decision to want change in our lives and accept Jesus as our Lord and Savior. Had not that happened, I would not be at the place I am today.

I have overcome many obstacles since that time, and I am grateful but still learning. I am much wiser and stronger in my faith and belief in who Jesus is and how much He loves us by sharing that love with others because of what He had done in my life. I was given the opportunity through my church to share my testimony with the world through TBN. It was a moment in time that I was so grateful to have known that a window was open from heaven to pour out a blessing on someone's life that needed to be blessed at that time, because this is life, and we are all going to experience different things as we journey on the road called life. So this is a part of my journey as I share with the world about how Jesus loves us unconditionally and He wants us to truly believe and trust in Him.

I know that might be hard for some of us to understand because we say it's easier said than done, but if you like to read books, I recommend that you start reading the Bible. And when you read, ask God for understanding as you read. I can assure you that you will start seeing things in a different perspective. I went back to what I was first taught from as a child the Bible after many years of trying to do and make things happen the way I wanted to, not knowing that I was already broken and could not fix the problem, only to realize that I need help. I needed the help of a Savior, and I began reading the Bible again, only this time I was being taught in a different way. What I was reading, I understood the true meaning of the cross and what it represented. That God had sent his Only Begotten Son into the world, that whosoever believed in him would not perish but have everlasting life (John 3:16).

It has helped me to help so many others in sharing the Gospel of grace, because all our lives is an open book. Just like the men and women of the Old and New Testament, we all have a story to tell that will help someone along the way to strengthen and encourage, to preserve and never give up hope. Believe in yourself and the one who created you.

Today I am so thankful that I have been reborn with unconditional love, a love that will never fail, because I get to share the love of Jesus. I have a women's prison ministry that I share with gratitude how the love of Jesus delivered me from that evil and dark place of addiction that once tried to cripple my life and destroy me. I was blessed to be a blessing to so many women who are going through and experiencing the trauma I had experienced on my journey through darkness. God has given me the ability to take back to those who are lost and share what He can do for us if we will give all to Him, and so He uses the ones who come to Him and acknowledge that they need His help.

To go back and help others, this is what I do today in my women's ministry: give strength to those who are weak, build them up where they are torn down, and to have hope, courage, and faith to continue on this journey, not to give up because Jesus has already paid the price for us and we have the victory over defeat. Revelation 12:11 (KJV) says, "And they overcame him by the blood of the Lamb, and by the word of their testimony; and they loved not their lives unto death." I am so grateful to serve in this ministry, because we all need each other down here. That is why we were put here to share the love of Jesus and to help each other along the way as believers.

We must all stand up for the righteousness of God through faith in what His Son, Jesus Christ, has come here and done, that we may continue to have the victory that is already ours in Jesus's name. I love sharing with my ladies, and I thank God for opening the door that I have, because they give me such great feedback to let me know how it's making a difference in their lives. So many of them have been down that destructive road of addiction, trying to find the right path. And to know Christ is a blessing beyond blessings. He will send guidance our way when we accept and believe in Him.

Chapter 6

Angels, Visions, Dreams, and Demons in the Natural and Supernatural Realm
A Letter from God

The Unbelievable That Took Place with
the Cross around My Neck

IN THIS CHAPTER, I SHARE my experience with the spiritual realm
through dreams, visions, angels, and demons. I have had encounters
with angels in the physical. I have had dreams and vision that were
manifested in my life. I know what I was dreaming and seeing was
very real; to my understanding, it's all a part of this journey on my
way to my destiny. Drugs and alcohol are destroyers; they are evil
spirits, demonic forces that are design to kill, steal, and destroy the
mind, soul, and body of mankind. There is no sympathy of feelings,
compassion, or love. It's all about your destruction. But to be reborn
in the spiritual is about having the God kind of life—a blessed life.

Angel 1

In the summer of 2006, I was at Ladies Only Total Fitness. Me and Ms. Delores were talking when out of nowhere, this beautiful little short lady came in the door with these long dreadlocks, very distinctive. I thought she was coming in for a workout, but instead, she then came over to me and my friend. We were sharing a conversation about military life. I myself am a veteran, and she was in agreement with us. Her conversation with us was brief. I noticed how she just kept her eyes on me, and then she said to me, "I want you to get this book called *The Four Agreements*, and read it."

After that, she left. She didn't say anything else, she just walked out the door. We continued to talk, but I wanted to ask her something, so I immediately went out behind her. When I looked for her, she was nowhere to be found. I went up and down the storefronts, asking if a short lady with dreads had come in here. No one had seen her. I knew I would have seen her if she was still around.

I went back to the gym and told my friend that I did not see her; I don't know where she went, but she was nowhere to be found. I went in every store looking for that little short lady with the dreads. We were both puzzled about how quickly she disappeared.

Then the thoughts that came to mind was that she must have been an angel, and being who I am today, a believer in Christ Jesus, having being taught from scriptures in Hebrew 13:2: "It is written be not forgetful to entertain strangers. For thereby some have entertained angels unaware." I knew that was an angel that came to me that day. I knew deep down within. At the time, I was not aware of her when she first approached me, but after it was over, I knew without a doubt in my heart that I had spoken with an angel that day.

I went and got the book. As I was reading it, my understanding was being opened to know wisdom that was within me. I knew what I experienced was real, and the book was very interesting after reading it. I went back some time later and read it again.

Today I am reading my notes, and now I am really understanding the wisdom that we have abiding inside us and how we can be an artist of our own life.

Angel 2

I was at the Gym LA Fitness, learning how to swim. I was using different types of swimming gear to help me stay afloat on the water. It was very helpful because I could swim just as if I were swimming without any help, thanks to my friend Patricia, better known as Trish. But anyway, the tools that I was using were very helpful, and I could see myself getting better and better. Because swimming was something that I had longed to do.

Then one evening, I was at the pool, and I had swim to the other end of the pool. I was standing there, catching my breath. While I was standing there, I saw this beautiful, slim, and very petite lady get into the pool. She was very poised. My eyes were drawn to her. I stood there watching her as she swam. Her strokes were amazing, so professional, and she only swam up and down one time, then she got out of the pool. She swam with such elegance I was determined to swim without any attachments because she had motivated me into doing it.

I don't know if she had been watching me as a swimmer, but I felt as if she had made a statement to me when she got in and got out. I felt like she was telling me in so many words to do it like this. I don't recall her looking at me. She just nicely got out of the pool. I don't remember seeing her walk away.

I took off my floater and walked down to the other end of the pool. I pushed myself off and started swimming and swimming and swimming. When I got to the other end, I stopped and looked back;

I was at the other end of the pool. I was so happy not to mention proud of myself. I did it, I swam without any attachments.

I went looking for her to share the good news of how she inspired me to let go and swim, and to let her know that I was determined after watching her. But she was nowhere to be found; it was like she disappeared. I went throughout the locker room looking for her, but she was nowhere to be found. Again, I knew that was my angel that had come to give me hope, encouragement, inspiration, and motivation. I was amazed as well as excited about my accomplishments of doing something that I thought would take me a long time to do. Although I was determined, I didn't expect to accomplish it so soon, and I did.

My story about swimming begin with a lady named Patricia, a water aerobics instructor who taught classes. She showed me the basics of swimming, and she offered to teach us how to swim. I had always wanted to learn, so with the door being open, I knew this was my opportunity to learn another one of the God moments to be recognized. I took advantage of the opportunity and begin learning the basics. She was a good coach who helped me with getting to where I am today. I practiced morning, noon, and night. I became obsessed with the idea of learning to swim. I would watch other swimmers as they would come into the pool and swim looking at their technique.

I was open for learning, and there were times when professional swimmers would come in and swim. I would get advice from them as they watched me swim, and so I was determined. But then in the end, this beautiful angelic being came at a time when it was only me in the pool. I will never forget that evening. It was special for me because the world had elected our first black president, and he was up for reelection, President Barrack Obama. He did win the election and served another four years as president of these United States (November 2008–2016).

That November evening, I took a giant leap of faith. I was happy and full of so much joy and excitement—so much so that I was bursting at the seams. I had learned how to swim without the help of the floater. I could not wait to get home and tell Al the good news that I did it.

He was so happy for me but was not surprised. He would always tell me, "You can do this, sweetie." He was my biggest fan and greatest supporter. He always believed in me when it came to challenges. He said, "I knew you were going to do it." He was my hero, and today when I swim, I swim for him too. He was a great swimmer. He would always say to me, "Sweetie, when you learn how to swim in four feet of water, then we are going to swim in ten feet." I said, "Okay, baby, I can't wait."

I thank Jesus for letting me discover the art and gift of swimming, that He allowed me to share with my friends and most of all the lady who showed me the way, my trainer and friend Patricia. And the angel who came in the end to give me the courage, confidence, and inspiration that I could do it, thank you for your help! Thank you, Jesus, for your angels. Philippians 4:13 says, "It is written: I can do all things through Christ who strengthens me."

I will always be grateful for the love and friendship we shared. You brought a lot of positivity in my life for being there with me when my husband went home to be with the Lord. You and Michael were the bridge that carried me over. The support and love were divined to one of the most caring and loving people I have ever met. I will forever be grateful for you both were my angels here on earth. Again, I say thank you and I love you!

At the cross where I first saw the blood!

This is a story that I must share. It is a miracle that took place. I will never forget that morning. I was living in East Point, Georgia.

We had recently just gotten our first apartment on June 2, 2006. It was quite the blessing, considering where I come from. It was my piece of heaven, someplace to live after spending years of being homeless with nowhere to call home. But then it all changed because I had a mind to want to change the way that I was living and to seek help. So I asked Jesus to come into my life and help me. Upon seeking His face, His Holy Spirit took total control of my every step, and I started walking in His guidance.

Things seemed to be balancing itself out for the good in my life, I had been blessed to have a place I could finally call home. I was in my bathroom getting ready one morning. As I was putting my makeup on, my eyes suddenly went to the cross that was around my neck. It was a 14-karat gold chain cross with Jesus hanging on it. As I was standing there, I could not believe what I was seeing: the cross had come to life, and it was showing the actual suffering and death of Jesus dying on the cross. It showed the blood dripping from the crown of thorns that was on his head. The blood, as I watched, dripped from his head and ran down the cross. It never dripped off the cross and on me, which I now wish that it had. This was such a phenomenal sight.

I starting hollering for Alton. He came running in to see what was going on. I told him to look at the cross around my neck and tell me what he sees. When he saw what was happening, his mouth was wide open. He could not say anything. We both were in shock as we looked at what was taking place in the bathroom mirror. There were times when the cross would enlarge itself. It was so real; I had never in life experienced anything like this, and I know had my life not changed, I don't think I would have had that encounter with the cross.

This lasted for quite some time. I was constantly going back to the mirror to see if it was still there. I will always cherish that moment; it was a special time for me and Alton. I often wondered why and what God was trying to show me about that vision and His Son. Since that day, I have received so many revelations and understanding about the cross that I no longer have to wonder anymore. I now know the reason he showed it to me. One of the many reasons is because he loved me so much that He gave his only begotten son, that whosoever believed in Him would not perish but have everlasting life (John 3:16).

It was truly amazing to see this cross that I had been wearing actually come to life, letting me know that the cross is real, and yes,

He died for my sins and was raised to life on the third day. I am a firm believer in the finished works of what Jesus came here and done for all humanity. The more I renew my mind in the Word and hearing the teaching about Jesus and the cross, it was confirmation on what was to come after seeing this. When we moved into our new home in July 2010, we experienced another astounding vision on the wall in our living room.

Showing Jesus hanging on the cross and the angels going up and down upon the Son of Man. The heavens were open, and there were the rainbow colors surrounding him. It was God-like glory like I never seen it before. The vision was just like the scripture said in John 1:51: it is written when Jesus said the truth is, you will all see heaven open and the angels of God going up and down upon the Son of Man.

I was amazed that when I read this after seeing the vision on that wall in my living room, we were so glued to the vision until we could not believe what we were seeing. That God had brought His Word into our living room, with me and my husband both witnessing the miraculous viewing of the heavens opening and angels going up and down upon the Son of Man.

I am so excited to know that Jesus was revealed to the both of us in our home. I had forgotten about the vision in our apartment with the cross that was around my neck that happened in 2006. Now I understand why I saw the vision: God was fulfilling what His Word said. And the amazing thing is that he was on the cross in both visions. He visited us in our apartment in 2006, and again in our home in 2010. It was at the cross that I surrendered my life, and I owe it all to you. Because of that cross, my sins were washed away, never to be remembered again. Then sing my soul, my savior God, to thee. How great thou art, how great thou art. Thank You, Jesus, for Your love, grace, and mercy! Yes, Jesus loves me for the Bible tells me so!!!

Seeing in the Supernatural and the Natural

Drugs and alcohol are destroyers. They are evil, demonic forces that are designed to kill, steal, and destroy the mind, soul, and body of mankind. I was once a stone-cold crack addict, addicted to drugs, alcohol, and cigarettes. These three are killers of the worse kind. These are the untold events about my battle and struggles when I was going through the things I had done. The places it took me and the people I encountered on the journey. I can only tell what I saw through the supernatural, the natural, visions, dreams, angels, and demons with the naked eye.

I have been visited by demonic forces in the Spiritual as well as the supernatural forces of the heavenly realm. Demonic forces are evil spirits that work against your spirit to keep control over you. I have had close encounters of the God kind and of the evil kind. These forces of evil make you lie, steal, cheat, rob, and kill. There is no sympathy, feelings of compassion, or love. It's all about your destruction. But to be reborn in the spiritual is about having the God kind of life a blessed life.

I can remember the time when I was asleep underneath an old rusty body of an eighteen-wheeler truck, which had been parked for years behind some old buildings. At the time, it was my "cat hole," which is the street name used for *housing*. I was asleep under the truck to be awakened by the heat and sweat that was pouring off me. As I sat up, I was sitting there, looking around. I saw this big long thing that looked like a snake. I wasn't sure at the time what I was looking at, but it wasn't the norm. What I saw was very terrifying and frightening because of the way it looked. But the most amazing part was that I was not afraid of what I saw, when I had every fear in the world to be afraid of what I was looking at. There were this peace and a sense of clam that were over me that would not let me be frightened or afraid.

Because what I saw and where I was at would have made the average person hurt themselves trying to get away or, even yet, have a heart attack in the process looking at the demon forces from hell. But not me. Only because the presence of God was there, and I was being covered by the blood of Jesus. He shut him down to where he could only look and not move. I don't know how long this thing (serpent) had been lying there watching me; all I know was when I sat up, this was what I encountered. It was the biggest snake I had ever seen. When I looked into the face, which looked like a human face, I saw it was round shaped, like a pie, with big round eyes. They were blood-red, and on each side of his face and mouth were whiskers, like a bobcat's.

I remember looking into the face of this creature, and it was staring back at me. I proceed then to go down the side of where he was lying at the time, upon some rusty iron crate boxes. He had a bird's eye view of me. I was trying to see how long it was. As I was looking, I saw it was very long. I would say it was over twelve feet long. It was black with silver stripes. I didn't see no end in sight.

I began to come back up, looking at this snake, and we then locked eyes again. Upon seeing those blood-red eyes staring at me, he closed them. I reached back, grabbed my wig, and crawled on my hands and knees from underneath that truck. Walked down the side and left from back there. Went back out front to join with the others, never speaking of what I had seen or encountered.

They would have thought I had been smoking some crack, and already being a serious crack head, to tell them that story I would have really been off my rocker. So for so long, I kept it to myself until one day, I told my then boyfriend what I had seen. I didn't think he was going to believe me, but to my surprise, he did. We never went back under that truck to sleep again. At the time, I should have been going through torture and a lot of excruciating pain. You would have thought I would be very intense or have lost my mind, but I was not and did not feel a thing. It's amazing when your eyes are open to the spiritual realm because you then see the good, the bad, and the ugly!

On July 31, 2018, my dad went home to be with the Lord. On December 24, 2018, I had a dream about my father. I was in this building; I don't know exactly what type of building, it looked more like at the time an old school building. I was standing in the hallway.

There were stairs and a door with a big picture window in it. The walls were of a gray color.

As I was standing there, I saw my father pass by the door. He was outside the building. As he passed by, he went into the room, and I could hear him talking with my mother. I didn't see her, but I knew it was her, and he was telling her that he was sorry for the way he treated her, and he asked her to forgive him. Then he left. As he was passing by the door, he looked through the window, as if he was looking for someone.

He saw me, opened the door, and came to me. I was so happy to see my dad. He came over to me and gave me a kiss on each of my cheeks, and then he turned and left. He never spoke a word. He looked young, radiant, and handsome, just like in the picture I have of him and Mother that they took together when they were younger. He had looked just like he did on this picture and had on the exact same suit that he has own in this picture.

I told my father that I was glad to see him. And his appearance was a sincere and serious-looking one. He turned and left back out the door he came in.

I woke up. It was Christmas Day. When I told my younger brother, Minister Todd Moser, about the dream he interpreted the dream telling me what that dream was about. I thank Jesus for the anointing on my brother's life.

The reason I am sharing this information in my story about the angels, visions, and dreams is because they are real and a part of my transformation, the change that has taken place, and they have played a major role in shaping my character and the person I have become today. Since the homegoing of my husband Alton, in April of 2013, my mother in February 2015, my father July 2017, my baby sister June 2018, my oldest brother January 2019, my younger brother Mark, July 2020 through it all, God has given me the strength to keep trusting and believing in him, knowing that His grace is sufficient to keep me. Even when I am feeling down and discouraged, I know by resting in him that all is well with me and my life. I have learned from renewing my mind in the Word; it gives me peace in the midst of the storm. While I was going through my addiction, I lost one of my younger brothers named Michael, and I did not know it until I connected back with my family. I was so hurt and heartbroken to hear that from Mom and Dad. I can just image what they went through behind the loss of their son and the fact that no one could find me to tell me the sad news. I often think of Michael, hoping that he is in heaven with Mom and Dad. I missed that homegoing, but I believe with all my heart that he is at home with the Father and my family.

My mother was such a powerful woman of God. She taught us to memorize the scriptures of the Bible, and in doing, so she was planting and nourishing the seed of God's words in our heart as children. As she got older, Momma became sick and was suffering from several medical issues, and because of the many struggles with her heart and diabetes, she started having amputation of the legs—first one and then the other—which led to prosthetics and a wheelchair.

I felt so sorry for Mom. I could not show my emotions with the way I was feeling around her. I had to be strong for my mom. There were times when I wish I could do more, but I couldn't. After being reunited with my family, I saw how my mother's health was declining.

I was thankful that I had come back at a time when I could be there for her to show my love and support. Just glad to be back into the lives of my family, being there for them as much as I possibly could. Although I lived in Atlanta, I would go home to Ruby, often to be close to her. I looked forward to seeing my mother because we were bonding again, and I would always bring her something beautiful to wear.

She looked forward to my coming home. I would fix her hair, give her a makeover, and dress her. She looked so beautiful when I finished with her. Then we would take pictures together. Now that Mom is gone, I have memories and pictures we shared together. I did what I thought and knew would make Mom smile and be happy, because my mother did not smile often anymore, she always looked sad and lonely. But to see her smile, it was beautiful; she was a beautiful woman. I know there were times when my mother wished she could get up and walk like she used to. But then we her children had become her feet when she needed help.

She would often remind us of how blessed we are to have feet until we no longer have them. She was facing the reality of change in her life, knowing that her life was forever changed. She had prosthetic legs, and from time to time, she would put them on when we would give her that boost of energy, and then there were those days when she didn't feel up to walking. Those prescription drugs that she was taking were making her weak, and in some cases, her body was becoming numb to the medication.

I can remember going home, and Mom was happy to see her children come home, especially the girls because we live in different places. I would make sure I went home to see my momma as often as possible. I had to make sure that my home and other responsibilities were taken care of before preparing to go. I no longer had my other half. It was heartbreaking to lose such an important part of your life. What a loss. I really had a hard time adjusting to life without him; it was very painful he was no longer with me.

But then I still had my mommy. Although she was sick, her mind was very strong and stayed that way until she departed this life. I could go home and be in her company; that was healing for me as well. It helped me get through my grief. I needed to be around my family. I was that little girl again, wanting her momma. I was so thankful that God had spared my life to be able to come back into my momma's life to help her. Being there for her was truly one of the greatest blessings that Jesus had given unto me. I was grateful that He had become a part of my life, which was forever changed.

I had become a new creation in Christ Jesus, thanks to His Word in 2 Corinthians 5:17 (KJV): "It is written therefore if any man be in Christ Jesus he is a new creature old thing are passed away, behold, all things are become new." I thank him for allowing me to connect back to the roots of my family. My mother was a very strong woman, and only wanted the best for her children. She loved us all and did the best she could.

There were times when my dad was not always supportive of the family as he should have, and this made my mother sad. Over the years, she became sick from worry and depression, which affected me greatly because that was my mother, and to have share my life and love with her was what I was looking forward to, after being separated for years. I just knew that I was going to be sharing a lot of good times with her.

Now that I had my family, she would be able to come and spend time with me whenever she wanted to. I looked forward to those times. Times that never happened because my mother's health was failing. She couldn't travel long distances, and so I always went home to be close to her.

This is what love is to me. Love is something very special to the heart and to have and to share; it's something that makes you a better person. Having understanding in all things and most of all the places it will take you. If you had to face fear or worry about going out into the world telling each soul about how much God loves you, that's what I would say love is. I looked forward to going home and being close to my mother, sharing the love that she had given me.

Before learning of Dr. Dollar and his teaching, my world was spiraling out of control. I didn't have a life. I was addicted to drugs and alcohol, and there was no relief nowhere in sight. I was making a lot of foolish turns and mistakes in my life. I did not know what I was getting myself into or just how dangerously I was living, not realizing that at any moment my life could be gone because of what I was doing, and where I was at sleeping outside wherever I could. It was very dangerous, even though I was in somewhat of a relationship.

Living that type of life was a very intense and destructive life. I became aware of Dr. Dollar in 2006. I was listening to him on television. And I liked what I was hearing; it was so real to me what he was teaching, and it was what I needed to hear and know at that time. I was getting answers to a lot of things that were going on with me. I was hungry for Jesus, and he was teaching about forgiveness of sin, the new covenant, believe and receive, eternal redemption, grace, for living. Today he talks about the balancing of faith and grace and how grace makes and faith takes, standing against strife, no imputation of sin.

All these teachings enlighten my understanding about the Gospel of grace and the benefits we have today being under the new covenant of grace. I could apply all of them to my life, because there was such a need for me to hear and know about my faith, belief, and how to live a victorious life in Christ Jesus. It was like an overnight sensation. I was amazed at how quickly my life was transformed because I knew what I was being taught was the right thing. Revelation, knowledge, and conformation were being given unto me. It was a great healing process for me and my husband.

The struggles and difficulties of life were not as important as my transformation that I had made. It was very well received once I understood the love of Jesus. The key moments that allowed me to make this transformation is the moment I realized I was at the place where the Holy Spirit had directed us to. My husband went home to be with the Lord, April 2013. But to know that he was at a place in life where he had accepted Jesus as Lord and Savior changed our lives forever. He was walking in the righteousness of God, set free from the addictions that once tormented his life. Not only his life but mine as well. He broke the chains that had us bound and set us on the right path so that the need for change could take place in our lives. It was at this point that it was time for me to hit the reset button, and to begin a new and a transformed life in Christ Jesus with a new identity.

What I want people and the world to gain from this book and my testimony is that there is hope, strength, and inspiration in whatever you are going through, but you have got to have a mind to want to change whatever is wrong in your life and accept Jesus as your

Lord and Savior. He is the only one who can fix whatever is wrong or broken in our lives and make it right. My advice to you and whoever you are reading my story, listen to me today: if you are caught up in these evils and are thinking about trying it, get out while you can. Don't waste your life on something that's not going to benefit you. You will always be a loser. Know that we are all winners in Christ Jesus; He has won the victory for us. I can assure you that these addictions will not help. They will destroy your life if you do not seek the help you need for change, because how we live makes all the differences in our lives.

Today I want to share some of my accomplishments, which are blessings from my Father since I have been under the teachings of grace. July 2010 I was blessed to own my first home ever. In February 2018 I will be seventeen years clean and sober from the addictions that once controlled by life. I am a 2015 graduate of World Changers Bible School, with an associate degree in Christian Studies, a certificate of completion in Pastoral Studies, a dean's Lister 3.50 to 3.99, a magna cum laude 3.70 to 3.89, and superlative awards.

This is what I want to share with others who are going through difficult times: if Jesus can deliver me from the hands of the enemy and give me a second chance in life, he will do the same for you. But you have got to want him and believe in what he has come here and done for us. I am truly amazed at the things that have taken place in my life from the beginning to end. I know there is a God and He loves us unconditionally.

What has inspired me the most throughout my journey is knowing today how much Jesus loves me. He loved me then, and he loves me even more today because I now love him. And as for my journey, I wouldn't change or take nothing for the life-changing experience because had it not been for the journey, I would not be able to share the good news of the Gospel of grace, and all the blessings that has come from him and how much it means to my life today. Sometimes God brings us to a place in our lives for such a time as this.

Halleluiah! Thank You, Jesus. Praise God, our Heavenly Father, for his son, Jesus. Because of the cross and his shed blood, we are not under the law but under grace.

Who am I outside the role I play is a person that was created to be the original copy? He has perfected everything that concerns me and is for me. My long-term goals in life is to write the book about my life, to become an inspiring motivational speaker, and to pursue my purpose here on earth in fulfilling my dreams and destiny, achieving my goals and accomplishments in life. My strengths are staying connected to my beliefs and faith centered around positive people and in a positive environment.

I no longer want to have to deal with my weaknesses, such as doubt and fear that something I am believing for will not happen, when I know that I have the right motives and I am in the right place and settings. My life will continue to go to heights unknown, because I know that I am doing the right thing by walking in faith, believing and receiving what Jesus has done for me. At this point in time in my life, I am where I am supposed to be.

How can I be sure I am in the right place and doing the right thing? Because I know and feel it and when you know and know you know, then you know it is right. Everything is in divine order. Which has been ordained form the beginning of time. I feel and know when I am centered around the right people, and Jesus is directing my steps as I go. It's like I said, it just feels right, and it amazes me the way things have taken shape in my life. It all seems to fit right into place. Whatever my purpose is, I know that it will be fulfilled by discovering who I am in Christ Jesus.

Therefore, it's so very important that I stay connected to positive people—people who want change in their lives with the same motives. Who wants to have a successful and fulfilling life of prosperity, a life pleasing to God. As I travel this journey, I want to discover the resources that are available for me to accomplish my goals. I have learned there are many resources. For starters, there is the Bible, the Internet, schools, churches, group settings, and the list goes on. Because technology is so plentiful today, we can have whatever we need and want right at our fingertips.

I am loving myself and the person that I am becoming very much, so I just want to keep getting better and better. There are so many things I want to achieve in this lifetime, knowing all the promises that God has promised me whenever I am faced with situations in my life that I know I cannot resolve alone. And these promises are a reminder through His Son, Jesus Christ. So that I can help others on this journey as we go through life. I want to be successful in every area of my life.

The goals that I have accomplished bring me the greatest joy. The fact of knowing that my life has been changed and I am a new creation in Christ Jesus. My life has really changed for the better, and the blessings that I have received through that transforming of the mind, it is awesome to know that I can accomplish whatever I put my mind to. Because in Philippians 4:13, it is written I can do all thing through Christ Jesus who strengthens me. My greatest joy is when I am victorious, meaning he has given me the victory to triumph over the enemy.

What I want people to know when they read about me is that I am passionate about pursing my goals and purpose in life, and being used by Jesus as he elevates me after going through that place of darkness and evil. By the grace of God, he delivers you.

It frustrates and saddens me today when I go home to my family and they do not want to accept the change that has taken place in my life. It makes me sad to see this because I really want to reach out and share the good news about how Jesus delivered me so that I may be a blessing to them by sharing my testimony. But see that you are being rejected by your family, and there is no growth, and every time I go home around my people, things are still the same and in some cases worse than before. It is very alarming, and it shows that there is no spiritual growth there anymore.

I know who you are because I grew up with you, remember, so you can't tell me anything that I don't already know because we were all raised in the church. So I pray for my family, especially those who are not saved, that Jesus will open their understanding and I move on with my life knowing that all is well.

At this time, I am where I need to be doing, what I am doing so that I can be ready, for I have always had a strong feeling deep down within that God is preparing me for wherever it is He is taking me. The mistakes were the experiences to get me there because it's going to take these trials and tribulations to strengthen me on my journey as I have said before sometimes God brings us to a place in our lives for such a time as this. This is a beautiful world full of beautiful people, places, and things. If I could live somewhere else, it would be very hard to decide. Because the things that I do and for the most part being involved with make me feel good and happy, because I see that my life is changing around me. I am growing and learning from it all at the same time. I truly am experience something that I know is a part of my journey.

My relationships with people are mutually beneficial and symbiotic. They are helpful as well as inspirational to others because of the transformation that has taken place in my life. And because of the change, there is always room for improvement. This is how I grow from being in interactive relationships with others. To be able to help people, I must accept and make room for improvement. I have accomplished and accepted transforming change in my life. From darkness to light, from lack, poverty, to prosperity. From homelessness into the everlasting arms of Jesus, who put me in a secure and beautiful home.

I have truly been blessed by the transformation that's taken place in my life. It has brought great understanding because of the love and sacrifice of my Lord and Savior Jesus Christ. Having him abiding inside me is all I need. But there is always room for improvement. There are times now when I look back and see where He has brought me from. If there was anything that I could go back and change, you know what? I wouldn't change a thing.

Had not I experienced it, I would not be the person I am today. I would not have been able to move forward and be a blessing to others and to the ones that are yet to come into my life. In closing out the chapters in this book, I want to share with you the letter that I received from God, and present this finale to me and my future, giving myself all the love and admiration that I deserve for staying the course and not giving up when things got tough. Because I was Reborn and He shared with me His Unconditional Love, A love That Never Fails.

 # A Letter from God

ONE DAY, I ASKED GOD why I never hear Him the way other people say they do. My question was, "Why you never talk to me like you talk to other people?" So He sent this letter to me to let me know that He, God, is talking to me, and this is my letter that God sent me. God is talking to you, my child. God is talking to you. Notice a scripture after each comment.

"You may not know me, but I know everything about you" (Psalm 139:1).

"I know when you sit down and when you rise up" (Psalm 139:2).

"I am familiar with all your ways" (Psalm 139:3).

"Even the very hairs on your head are numbered" (Matthew 10:29–31).

"For you were made in my image" (Genesis 1:27).

"In me you live and move and have your being" (Acts 17:28).

"For you are my offspring" (Acts 17:28).

"I knew you even before you were conceived" (Jeremiah 1:4–5).

"I chose you when I planned creation" (Ephesians 1:11–12).

"You were not a mistake…all your days are written in my book" (Psalm 139:15–16).

"I determined the exact time of your birth and where you would live" (Acts 17:26).

"You are fearfully and wonderfully made" (Psalm 139:14).

"I knit you together in your mother's womb" (Psalm 139:13).

"And brought you forth on the day you were born" (Psalm 71:6).

"I have been misrepresented by those who don't know me" (John 8:41–44).

"I am not distant and angry, but the complete expression of love" (1 John 4:16).

"And it is my desire to lavish my love on you" (1 John 3:1).

"Simply because you are my child and I am your Father" (1 John 3:1).

"I offer you more than your earthly father ever could" (Matthew 7:11).

"For I am the perfect Father" (Matthew 5:48).

"Every good gift that you receive comes from my hand" (James 1:17).

"For I am your provider and I meet all your needs" (Matthew 6:31–33).

"My plan for your future has always been filled with hope" (Jeremiah 29:11).

"Because I love you with an everlasting love" (Jeremiah 31:3).

"My thoughts toward you are countless as the sand on the seashore" (Psalm 139:17–18).

"And I rejoice over you with singing" (Zephaniah 3:17).

"I will never stop doing good to you" (Jeremiah 32:40).

"For you are my treasured possession" (Exodus 19:5).

"I desire to establish you with all my heart and all my soul"(Jeremiah 32:41).

"And I want to show you great and marvelous things" (Jeremiah 33:3).

"If you seek me with all your heart, you will find me" (Deuteronomy 4:29).

"Delight in me and I will give you the desires of your heart" (Psalm 37:4).

"For it is I who gave you those desires" (Philippians 2:13).

"I am able to do more for you than you could possibly imagine" (Ephesians 3:20).

"For I am your greatest encourager" (2 Thessalonians 2:16–17).

"I am also the Father who comforts you in all your troubles" (2 Corinthians 1:3–4).

"When you are brokenhearted, I am close to you" (Psalm 34:18).

"As a shepherd carries a lamb, I have carried you close to my heart" (Isaiah 40:11).

"One day I will wipe away every tear from your eyes" (Revelation 21:3–4).

"And I'll take away all the pain you have suffered on this earth" (Revelation 21:3–4).

"I am your Father, and I love you even as I love my son, Jesus" (John 17:23).

"For in Jesus, my love for you is revealed" (John 17:26).

"He is the exact representation of my being" (Hebrews 1:3).

"He came to demonstrate that I am for you, not against you" (Romans 8:31).

"And to tell you that I am not counting your sins" (2 Corinthians 5:18–19).

"Jesus died so that you and I could be reconciled" (2 Corinthians 5:18–19).

"His death was the ultimate expression of my love for you" (1 John 4:10).

"I gave up everything I loved that I might gain your love" (Romans 8:31–32).

"If you receive the gift of my son Jesus, you receive me" (1 John 2:23).

"And nothing will ever separate you from my love again" (Romans 8:38–39).

"Come home and I'll throw the biggest party heaven has ever seen" (Luke 15:7).

"I have always been Father and will always be Father" (Ephesians 3:14–15).

"My question is…will you be my child?" (John 1:12–13).

"I am waiting for you" (Luke 15:11–32).

Now, you have God talking to you through the Holy Scripture.

Love,

Your dad, Almighty God!

I love you too, Dad. Yes, I will forever be your child. Thank you for saving me. You are an awesome Father, and I love you with all my heart, soul, mind, strength and body. I am so glad that I heard from you, because it makes me feel good let me know that you were listening to my grumbling and complaining, knowing that you are the Omniscient God who has perfect knowledge of all things. A Father who knows what we are thinking before we think it.

I love the way you responded back to me. It really opens me up to see how great and powerful you are. I want to fulfill the highest, truest expectation of my calling in life, knowing who I am. Learning from my mistakes, discovering as I travel this road on my way to my destiny what my purpose is. I know that everybody is not going to like me, and that's okay too. I am always surrounded by the right people who will inspire me, motivate me, give me hope and encouragement and inspiration.

I always want excellence to be the motivation point in knowing that I can do all things through Christ Jesus because of who I have become today. That was true strength and inspiration that you gave me in your conversation piece, along with your Word that I may read and meditate on each day. Just reading what you were saying to me was like I was hearing your voice speaking to me. I know this may sound weird to my readers, but that is the way I receive your answer, hearing you as I was reading. And having scripture to read behind your response? That is powerful.

There have been moments when I would be sharing your Word, and I would read a verse that sounded as if I heard you speaking to me through your Word. I now know that you do because you answered me back and made sure I received this important letter. I truly was blown away when I started reading this because nobody but God could answer my questions the way you did. For me to be able to immediately comprehend was truly divine.

There are just not enough words to describe how I feel at this moment, place, and time in my life. You know, Father, ever since I accepted you as my personal Lord and Savior, there have been some awesome changes in my life. The transformation has been unbelievable—blessings upon blessings. I never knew my Heavenly Father loved His children the way you do, until I accepted you as my Lord and Savior and became a believer. Even when we don't love you, You are still there protecting your children.

Thank you, Daddy, for loving me enough not to leave me the way I was. I will be forever grateful to your love, kindness, and tender mercy. Your daughter, Althea Driver!!!!!

Conclusion

Reborn Unconditional Love: A Love That Never Fails

MY LIFE IS AN OPEN book. I cannot begin to tell myself how proud I am of you and the great accomplishments, trials, and tribulations that you have been faced with. You showed strength, courage, and determination to stay the course. You had an awakening from your Heavenly Father that changed the course of your life forever. That was the vision that you wanted change. The light had stepped in and the darkness disappeared.

I am thankful that in looking back you never wanted to go back to that dark and evil world. You remembered the pain and hurt you suffered and from whence Jesus came and delivered you. He has broken the chains that once held you captive. You are no longer bound. You have been set free by the blood of Jesus, the precious Lamb of God. You are a strong, confident woman. Keep believing in yourself and the one who sent, made, and created you to know that there is nothing impossible for God to do. You can do all things through Christ Jesus who strengthens you (Philippians 4:13).

My dreams and goals are to be who God created me, to be whatever He has designed for my life. On this journey to my destiny is what I look forward to achieving and fulfilling in His strengths and power. I step it up because our time is getting short here. I love you, Kool, as you are. Know that you were created for a reason and a purpose. You have been reborn to die to your old self and reborn to your new self! Reborn love never fails.

After my death, I want future generations to know that our legacy is determined by what we leave others may I leave in others to have a heart for God. I lived a life of hope and inspiration to inspire so many, that the generations to come will know that I once existed and the person that I was through my seed toward others. I hope people will remember me as a loving, kindhearted person who walked in the favor and love of Jesus and His righteousness. Making a mark that cannot and will not be erased.

Reborn love never fails.

About the Author

ALTHEA C. DRIVER, BORN ON June 29, 1956 communicates the character of Christ through the Word of God in practical ways that engage her readers. Currently residing in Atlanta, Georgia, Althea Driver is the author of *Reborn Unconditional Love: A Love That Never Fails*. She joined the United States Army from July 9, 1974, to July 9, 1975, and she served at the VA Medical Center in Atlanta, Georgia.

From 1999 to 2001, Althea graduate from World Changers Bible School, where she completed a two-year associate degree program in Christian studies on April 4, 2015. She obtained a certificate of completion in pastoral studies, and she achieved a certificate of honor, making the dean's list. Althea graduated magna cum laude.

Althea is currently a member of World Changers Church International, where she sits under the teaching of Pastor Creflo and Taffi Dollar. Her life has made a mark that can never be erased, affording her the opportunity to share her testimony on Trinity Broadcasting Network (TBN) on December 31, 2017.

Althea wants her readers to know emphatically, as she stated, "I write to encourage others to take a leap of faith in pursuit of the God-given gifts and talents in which we have all been entrusted. I know who I am today, and I am eternally grateful."